Babaji
The Beginning Has No End

Cover illustration by Marcia Diane, Copyright © 2005
Cover Design by Victor Cebollero and Leslie Owens
Text Format by Victor Cebollero
Editing by Tula Flaouto, Jan Mosso, Calvin Odom, Charlie Siegel
and Matt Silver
Indexing by Phyllis Brown

The author would like to express his deepest appreciation to all those Masters, seen and unseen, who contributed immeasurably to this book, both in content as well as in the inspiration for it being written.

The author of this book does not dispense medical advice or prescribe the use of any techniques as forms of treatment for physical or medical problems without the advice of a physician, either directly or indirectly. The intent of the author is only to offer information of a general nature to help you in your quest for emotional and spiritual well-being. In the event you use any of the information in this book for yourself, which is your constitutional right, the author and the publisher assumes no responsibility for your actions.

For more information about the author, please visit
www.thewayoftruth.org

Babaji
The Beginning Has No End

by Michael Edward Owens

Introduction

It is my privilege and pleasure to write this introduction on the dialogues of Babaji. I have admired this great avatar throughout my many lifetimes. He has been a dear friend and mentor whose help has been invaluable in my leadership of the path of Light and Sound, The Way of Truth. Babaji taught me how to examine and use the chakras in the movement of consciousness outside the body called "Universal Soul Movement."

Babaji also initiated the awakening of my spiritual training in the physical realms. It was this great avatar that introduced me to my later mentors and teachers of old: Kadmon, Agnotti, and Milati. These spiritual masters have been my advisors since the beginning of my spiritual journey.

It was Babaji's intention to give those who know and love him a book that provides creative responses to the issues of love, family, work and daily life. Consequently, this book discusses spirituality in a way unique to other books on Babaji. What I found extremely effective for daily living were the contemplative exercises he offers in this book to expand the God seeker's sphere of love and knowledge. The words used as mantras (words of prayer) are phonetically charged with love and Light and Sound. The meaning of certain phraseology in the contemplative exercises is written to transcend the intervention of the mind.

I have used terminology entrenched in the olden ways of the spiritual, like Sugmad, also known as God. This term was used due to its structural integrity, and it has never been profaned in human language and verbal communication. Thus, the vibration to the word "Sugmad" has never been depleted or violated.

As the Living Teacher of The Way of Truth, I am called a Sehaji Master. The term "Sehaji" means "master of the celestial seas" alluding to the Ocean of Love and Mercy, the home of God's consciousness. This book was not intended to recruit or to propagandize the teachings of The Way of Truth, but there are references made to it throughout this book. The intersection of Babaji's spiritual teachings and that of The Way of Truth was inevitable to merge into one another. In essence, the foundations of both ways of life are integrally related to the beauty of God's love for all life and the freedom of Soul.

I believe you will find this book spiritually uplifting and of practical use in matters of spiritual inquiry. Many doors of perception and adventure await the God seeker who reads this book, uses the contemplative exercises and follows the path inside this book. The truth unveiled in this book is like the light shining brightly at the end of the tunnel.

Many Blessings, Sri Michael Owens

Preface

This book is the result of extensive training and rigorous evaluation from spiritual masters who have served Spirit in many capacities. The words and sentence constructs contained in this book reflect truths through a state of consciousness which relatively few have achieved. Articulation of truth from levels of reality far beyond the physical realm will often incorporate run-on sentence structures that convey energies to be experienced and not necessarily readily interpreted mentally. Open your heart to experience the wonderful flow of love, compassion, and kindness from Babaji.

CONTENTS

Carry well the knowledge that you are of the highest honored ones to usher in the greatest love to be seen in a millennium.

Chapter One

The Meaning of this Book

Babaji

*If one looks through the eyes of
the selfless heart, the explanation
for all in existence shines
brightly in the center of your
being.*

The Beginning Has No End

Babaji

"The beginning has no end" is the simplest way to say that the spiritual seas can never be completely traveled in a single lifetime. Embarking upon this journey to grow closer to the heart of God is a continuous blessing that we receive for Soul and for the prosperity of this universe. As we adventure into the God Worlds to seek our individual Mastership, we bring with us the energy of all souls who have ever taken a step towards God, the Light and Sound, or Spirit. In these efforts, the hearts of many individuals open their love, which is the most significant tool for the God seeker. Every action, every thought should be infused with love.

Once the journey has begun, the limitless worlds of the higher realms glisten with the new vibration of this soul energy that comes from the transition process in this universe that began with the African renaissance. As for the need for explanation within this book, Babaji, <u>The Beginning Has No End</u>, it is to bring a new light of hope to those who had only seemed to have accomplished a spiritual goal that was placed before them by other ways of life. The God seeker grows continually in the love of our Creator and guides others to this wondrous experience of being that is brought about by the joy of the open hearts that fill The Way of Truth.

Why Babaji is now speaking to us through The Way of Truth

Yours is a mission of great merit. I, Babaji, an acknowledged Master in the way of the Light and Sound, say to you that you have opened the consciousness of many souls to this new beginning. I offer my assistance and blessings to this journey in all ways. As before, in my journeys as a Master to many others that have brought the message of love to the hearts of those that sought to feel the presence of God on this Earth, I have laid down a foundation of spiritual interest that has been hidden from the hearts of many, but once again is being felt in this universe.

Babaji

The key for this compelling process of enlightenment is that the Light and Sound in this universe has gained a new strength. It has been felt in many of the higher realms of beingness. You in The Way of Truth have changed the frequency to make it more available to all souls that are being awakened in your efforts to please this Sugmad. The souls that have flocked to the entrances of these new vortices of spiritual energy will truly find the beginning that has no end.

It is a necessity in this Sugmad to join all prior and future efforts to sing out to all souls that God is ever present in all of them, if they seek love amongst all people and ways of spiritual awakening. In years past, the message has been placed in the hands of many devout people who were led astray by the intensity of the new God power that has been placed in this universe. They sought to direct it in the ways of the mental body and ego, and not through the way of the sacred heart. As I saw these things beginning to happen, I asked the great Overlords of this universe to provide a release valve for this restrained energy. They could also see the constriction of the Light and Sound, and the uncomfortable state of being in Sugmad's heart as souls were being held back from experiencing this wondrous love of life and spirit. The Way of Truth was set before the council, and a representative was selected in Dan Rin (the spiritual name of Sri Michael Owens), who, once put through a rigorous cleansing and training, was offered and accepted the honor of bringing this new balance to all souls who seek the true, selfless love in the God Worlds, and wish to share Sugmad's grace in all expressions of spiritual life.

It is for you to take hold of this God power and, through the Light and Sound, process that which is in transformation into an accessible set of new engrams that all willing souls may take this journey. The clarity of the Light of God in your heart will shine brightly as in times of old, when angels spoke directly to all souls of the open, selfless heart who knew of and sought a connection to God's love in this universe.

The Beginning Has No End

A gift from God to all living things

God's love is something that is present in everything in existence. To try and separate it and call it something other than the Light of the Spirit is the karmic process that Soul is thrown into in the worlds of duality. Soul is awakened to its true purpose in being- that is, giving realignment to the lower bodies and bringing expressions of love to all through the touch of the Living Master of the Light and Sound. All the ways that God's love permeates this universe are open to the eyes of the soul through the selfless heart of joy that is placed in each and every living thing in this existence. To separate human love from the love of God is to have a universe where the moon does not reflect the light of the sun. The joy of beingness, without the love of God, is as empty as the night sky without the moon and stars. God's love guides us even in the darkest times of our karmic responsibilities in the worlds of duality. Our Creator's love is the sustaining force beyond and through creation. It is the force behind the deeds that we may try and claim as our own doing. The spirit of God's love is all-sustaining to every way of life, and is the quantum singularity that draws all souls to Sugmad's grace and open heart.

When we maintain the attitude that what we share with one another is always a reflection of God's love, it keeps Soul in a state of balance with the truth of beingness. The Light and Sound is the gift of God's love returned to the consciousnesses of all souls in this time of universal change. The greatest gift we offer is the ability to share this joy through our every action and waking moment, so that as we breathe, we love.

How and why Soul awakens at seemingly the right time to work out its karmic cycle

When you find yourself awakened by the situations in life that seem to bring you to a place of awareness that God has a purpose for you in this universe, you have seen the end of karmic retribution in your life. This is a new freedom of Soul, to once again express the true love that Sugmad has placed in the center of your being. All that transpires in this universe is an act of God's love for us. As we take the action to once again live in the heart of God, all that is karmically linked to our action is purified and set aside. This is the power of love; this is the duty that is placed before you to take others away from the old ideas of living out a life of karmic debts. Let the Light and Sound shine through your heart for those souls yet unaware of this great love that will bring them into this time of God's grace.

Babaji's mission and how it coincides with the karmic cycle of this planet and this universe

Within my heart I have seen the need to bring this planet out of its karmic cycle by the awakening of God-Realization that has taken place in Abuja, Nigeria in Africa. This is the time that was set forth by the Lords of Karma to set free these people and to bring a new intensity of hope to your world. To re-ignite the hearts of these spiritual giants is to send a message to all realms of being that Sugmad's great love is awakened in this world, and is to be brought to all those who have suffered under the oppression of the dark lords for the past millennium. In my early teaching of the love of God, the voices of my disciples could only reach a few who searched, but as this great renaissance is taking place, many hearts are being drawn into the center of Sugmad's love as the new frequency of the Light and Sound is increasing the number of God-Realized beings in this universe. This movement is one that cannot be swayed from its course. It is filled with love from all ways of being, even those not yet aware of the Light and Sound that fill their hearts today. This planet's position in the awakening of this Sugmad is at the peak vibration of all Sugmads, and is the trumpeting of the new opening to the God Worlds for all those souls who have waited for this since the beginning of time.

The Beginning Has No End

Why God created what is now in this universe

If one looks through the eyes of the selfless heart, the explanation for all in existence shines brightly in the center of your being. When you question observations with the mental body, the joy of living is placed on a road that winds through a long karmic process of being until Soul, once again, becomes awakened to the true joy of beingness, in all realms above and below. This is the discovery of love for all things in this universe.

Sugmad has given us a truly great capacity for love and a thirst to share it, and only when we stand in the shadows of doubt and misunderstanding do we lose our way towards this great joy of God's love. Let your heart see the grace of caring for each other in this world of seeming chaos. Take the lens of illusion away from your inner sight; let the Light and Sound guide your journey back to the heart of Sugmad.

God's interchange with Its creation in this universe is one of the many expressions that It has had through many existences. Each time that Soul begins this journey, the joy that it brings to the heart of God is multiplied and sent out to all other planes of existence. It brings together the wonders that make love happen to each and every Soul awakened to the great spirit of being that is this universe.

Babaji

Chapter Two

Self-Realization

To experience self in a realized state of awareness is the first essence of God Knowing that has been planted in every Soul that experiences the love of Sugmad.

The Beginning Has No End

The nature and purpose of Self-Realization

When consciousness is awakened in the heart of an individual, a sense of the world around them begins to draw their attention to the division that seems to be present in their perception of things and their place in it. This could be considered the first awareness of self − when one realizes that there is an invisible connection to all life they had been unaware of until something inside of them began to shine like a small light on an area of consciousness that had been clouded. The subtle change in what someone of limited awareness begins to surmise is that there is something within that is calling out for recognition in this life. What they feel is not something that comes to the mind with an explanation of why it exists, it is more like a tap on the shoulder to say that it has always been there waiting to bring a new feeling of belonging to the individual. To raise the consciousness to see self is a simple step, but not many find it when they begin to search through philosophical and religious materials. The mental body tends to say that it can explain these feelings that lead to questions in the heart of the individual who, though coming into beingness, is still unaware. This journey leads this newly-awakened consciousness to the door of a path begins a wonderful journey within to seek out the meaning of this new sense of being that has been emerging in the heart. I use the word "awakened" rather than to say that it is born to the individual because the love of God is something that is and has always been, and when the heart is awakened − which always occurs at the designated time in the evolution of the consciousness of God − one more piece of the cosmic awareness of the Creator is put into place: the true display of the great love that God has in Itself for all Life.

What is about to take place is an expression of self that is a part of God's love in this individual, bringing it closer to God's heart because this is the road that we all must travel at some time in our existence. The urge to return home to the heart of Sugmad is the overwhelming energy that is the Light and Sound manifested in this and all universes far and wide - those universes that have been and those that will be. The need to broaden this new found awareness into active consciousness will bring the self to search for an understanding. The teachings of the mystery schools can ignite the fire of this search for the universal wisdom within that leads all to the heart of God. This substance that we know of as Sugmad (God) is a pure representation of love. For it to be shared from the center of the heart of the Creator, a spiritual hierarchy has been constructed over past eons of time and cycles of Sugmads. The great beings that have emerged from the wisdom of God's experience of Its own love are returned to us in the form of Masters. These Masters guide the Children of Light through the cycles of being as they grow toward the complete consciousness of God that is a part of their true beingness. How this search differs from what is offered in the religions of the world is that these Masters do not teach punitively. They offer gentle guidance through love and they take the individual through the many perplexing experiences that the newly-awakened self will endure as it walks to the realization of its beingness in God's heart.

What I am saying is that the religions of the lower worlds have lost the true essence of the Light and Sound (Spirit of God) and have replaced it with the egoistic need of domination over souls that seek only to be reunited with God's great love. This is veiled by punitive measures for disobedience and so-called rewards for good behavior, so often written into the text and doctrine of their theology. The true nature of this universe is the binding of love, which is the great force that fuels all desire for connectivity between all beings. Out of the chaos of the lower worlds and the simple awareness gained through the lower senses, the self is awakened to its existence through the effort of God's love of Itself in all things. As the self begins this journey to its awakening, it will find that there is light and love in everything that is visible, and for the first time the heart begins to see those things that have been veiled by lies and the illusions of the lower worlds of duality. It sees that love is the key to Self-Realization, soon to be understood as only a stepping stone to the great reunion that is about to occur. The move toward higher frequencies of love and light is just beyond the disappearing veil of ignorance. As the sight is tuned to the vision of God through the awareness of love, the ever-expanding heart is filled with the Spirit (the Light and Sound) that travels through this universe. You are Its children and are of Its own Self, and you will feel this even more as your heart grows pure in your search for truth and light. To experience self in a realized state of awareness is the first essence of God Knowing that has been planted in every Soul that experiences the love of Sugmad.

The nature and purpose of God-Realization

The immense nature of the love in this universe will not allow itself to be explained or expressed in the simple forms of consciousness that exist below the Great Divide. It is the nature of the illusion to hide and disguise this love to perplex the inner being of Soul so that Soul experiences the search for its unity with God, the origin of all beingness and love. Once realized, Self, as it wanders through the lower consciousness of being and guided by the mental body (ego), may come to the conclusion that it has reached its pinnacle of awareness, and assume that this is all it can aspire to be. The center of creation is unattainable through any process of lower awareness taught in other paths of life. The never-ending search for the true heart of selflessness is awakened on the path of The Way of Truth. What is sought by Soul is the connection to the great love that is drawing all life toward its beginning. This is seen in the realms below as the end as Soul passes out of the physical form, but within the God Worlds is known as the beginning of true existence in the heart of Sugmad. This is the best explanation that I offer for the journey into God-Realization at this time, for the many questions that this step of consciousness brings will gradually, through this book, be made clearer than ever before. The God Worlds are awaiting the return of the many souls that have been sent to gather the love that has been spread across many Sugmads, and to once again bring all the hearts of God's children together, as the beginning of the great new expansion of love is near. To be God-Realized is to be one with the immense love that drives all energy in existence. Once entered into, what is laid before Soul is the vision of itself at the beginning of its time in the heart of the Creator. This is an understanding that takes many life cycles to maintain and bring back to those parts of God that are waiting - those who have not yet accepted the light that is within each of them. God-Realization is a part of this cosmic puzzle that will no longer be veiled to the open, wanting heart of pure love and those devoted to the spreading of the Light and Sound through the universes of all Sugmads. God-Realization brings a new beginning to the soul heart center that shows the way to become a perfect conduit for the grace of God's love for all things. It will not take actions set forth by mental endeavors to bring a greater consciousness to self. It will transpire as the heart becomes transparent and allows the fire of Sugmad to burn brightly and drive the desires of all inhabitants of this universe and beyond.

As you travel in these realms of knowingness, I have laid before you the right tools of expression. They are found in the new teaching that the Sehaji have offered, and will greatly enhance the God Consciousness that is growing in your heart as we speak. All that shall come to pass in this time of beginnings has been prepared for by my many other disciples that have come before you. They have ignited the awareness of many souls that still slumber, caught in the mind's illusion that Self-Realization is the highest spiritual expression, and forever mired in the causal and astral trap of karmic re-evaluations. As the Lords of Karma have agreed to work with Dan Rin in moving more souls to the higher realms of God beingness, this has raised the frequency of love that fills this universe. Those souls that move with the grace of Sugmad as their guide, experience a release from the age-old process of karmic repetition that nearly brought the growth of this Sugmad to a halt. It is now the time to release these souls from bondage to join the choirs of hearts that sing praise to the love and manifestation of the

The Beginning Has No End

God power in realms below the Great Divide. This is the true nature and purpose of God-Realization in these times.

The difference between Self-Realization and God-Realization

Self has a limited view of the abilities of God's love in this universe, which is to say that it works only with the singleness of the mental consciousness of a seeker. God-Realization brings the Soul into direct contact with the God power of the universe, and, for all who look to the higher realms as a way of living in the worlds below, it allows them to draw into their hearts the grace of complete understanding. As this energy is moved across the Great Divide to awaken more of my children to the great love that can be shared, the heart of Sugmad shines ever more brightly to those that look to this universe as a guide to living in heart consciousness. Acting through the transparent heart of the pure God seeker is the power of the Light and Sound to transform those who strive to move beyond the self, and to help them realize and move beyond the mental body process that has been taught as the goal of the spiritual.

To raise this awareness has taken the slow process of re-awakening souls a few at a time to maintain the balance that is inherent in the universal laws. But at this time of renaissance in the Spiritual Seas, the blending of all forces above and below the Great Divide is seen everywhere as the new Light and Sound that can penetrate the heavy veil which has slowed this awakening for a millennium. As it has been said many times in the teachings of The Way of Truth, the cooperation of all spiritual Masters is offered to bring souls into the true heart of God in this cycle. To leave behind the limited awareness of Self-Realization in exchange for the compelling experience of God-Realization or the complete awakening of Soul to its true nature and its place in Sugmad's heart is to increase the flow of the new frequencies of love and deepen the presence of the Light and Sound in all realms of beingness. The self only carries the aspiration of Divine Love, whereas the God-Realized self in

Soul is this love manifested, and can heal and transform the many other souls that search for their home in God's heart. To begin to share this goal is the first step to differentiating between Self-Realization and God-Realization. The need to show this view of being to those who see a higher truth within themselves, is why the process of Self-Realization was first introduced to spiritual seekers in other cycles of spiritual growth through the ages. What transpired was the growth of the ego in some who lost their way. In Maya they became seduced by the inherent power of the illusion of oneness in the shadows of ignorance projected by the dark forces decades ago. The call to all souls to once again awaken and continue on to their true beginnings of love in Gods' heart has shone a brilliant light into the shadows and illuminates the way to those once lost in their selfish goals. This Sugmad will be complete as the great combination of God-Realized souls is blended with the new Light and Sound to draw all who lagged behind closer to God's heart.

Why Self-Realization is only half of Soul's journey home to God

For those guided towards the God Worlds there is a duty to pass karmic exercises. The need for education about things of a coarse nature found in the lower realms is necessary for showing the importance of balance in every step taken toward the God Self. Soul being suddenly awakened to its God being has caused many to wander lost in the cycles of reincarnation. They feel they need to perform some special task to be worthy of the love that they have received. This gentle step through Self-Realization has become the point of awakening Soul to the fact that God's love is supreme in this and all universes, and is the rightful gift that is offered by all Sugmads to Their children, to be shared with one another until we all stand united in the center of creation. From this place we will draw all souls into this great vortex of love and God power, so as to take this universe to its next level of expression in the vast sea of creative energy that is God's true love. The preparation needed to move from self, to Soul, and then to God Awareness has been placed in the hands of the Sehaji Masters who have chosen Dan Rin to place this new balance and presence of God's love into action. This has created a new vibratory frequency in the Light and Sound for many more to see across the Great Divide. In this way and at this time, I felt it was necessary to let this message of understanding come to you through the teachings of The Way of Truth. Since time immemorial, I have sought only to let you know of the greatness of God's love for all, and that sharing this love unconditionally is the first step into the God Worlds. To realize self is the only way to become selfless, and God's love is truly an expression that comes through the transparent, selfless heart of those who live in Its being.

The time of questioning has given way to the time of action, and the action is the sharing of your true self as Soul in the consciousness of God-Realization. This has been set before many of the Masters and has been given to you through them to take across many universes and Sugmads. For me to say that this is your time, is to awaken in you the need to satisfy the blending of the Light and Sound into useful frequencies for all to see and feel. We have been placed in newly-created levels of awareness and initiation, by this Sugmad, to present the love of all to those coming to this universe to replenish themselves in the pure waters of this Sugmad.

Why Soul was placed in a physical shell to discover its eternal nature

It is natural to ask this, for I have touched on it briefly before. The preparation for Soul's journey of consciousness has to be seated in a sustainable vehicle, and in this universe, your mortal shell was evolved for this purpose. Within its cellular electro-magnetic resonance is planted the seeds of discovery for its origins and the connection to something greater that defines its true beginnings. Has it not been said that the mortal shell is a microcosm of God's great cosmos? In this the Soul is tempered for the karmic activity that brings it strength and understanding when put to the tests of Kal Niranjan and the Lords of Illusion. For Soul to become completely aware of its true being, it must see that all is a part of its reality. To truly understand the immortality of God, the illusion of mortality was placed upon us. Why we sought for so long to define this existence in the small arena of self, was the way we have been lead to the limitless consciousness of God Awareness. In the evolution of the Light and Sound, the secret of our eternal self as God is shared when the heart becomes open at the first touch of God's love in the karmic life of self before it is realized. Once that threshold is crossed, the heavens literally open before the inner vision to reveal the limitless glory of the true universe of love and caring for one another. We must take part in these waters of pure fire that bring to those not yet awake the gentle, yet much needed cleansing of the mind's vision to see into their hearts where the true sense of being awaits their acceptance.

The vision of the Self-Realized being only sees the limited horizon of its daily experiences in the fulfillment of its heart's desire. It has not yet experienced its true heart-of-hearts to know that there is an opening to a greater sense of being just beyond the veil of contentment that it perceives as its goal in life. If the correct vibratory exercises are practiced as the self continues to evolve, it will awaken the force of singularity of Sugmad's love and will be guided forward to the next level of consciousness of love. The many other gifts that come at this time, present to the newly-emerged Soul the knowledge of its contract with this universe. Its need to understand this duty increases as the desire to grow and seek its home in God's infinite love fills the heart. Life takes on a new glow, and all things encountered seem to have a new meaning in accordance with the higher laws of Sugmad which are intuitively transmitted to the newly opened heart through the Light and Sound.

The Beginning Has No End

How God-Realization affects the individual consciousness

When Soul is awakened and the heart is opened by the divine touch of the Light and Sound, then the complete change in the consciousness and life work of the seeker begins. I have presented to many the joy of selfless acts of love and kindness as the road to true God-Realization, and the miraculous outcome in their lives is always the same – an opening of the heart and all other chakras that increase the flow of the Light and Sound, and the flow of the purest energy from God's love for all humanity. This is released through the heart of those who embrace the great God Consciousness that selfless love brings into this universe. The sense of belonging to the greater, as a selfless being, is part of the replaced attitude of Soul as it begins to work with God to bring greater understandings of love to all creatures. God's work is done when we live in this God-Realized state of existence, but when we look to the self for recognition, we take a brief step backward which gives a view of how great the non-power, the God power truly is. It has replaced those ideas of the mental body and ego with a sense of a transparent, selfless beingness in the heart of Sugmad. Soul is drawn to acts of love without thought, and presented with opportunities to be of service to many in the smallest ways. A connection to all humanity forms in the heart; there is a sense of purity in all the inner bodies, and new-found energy emanating from all the chakras. There is a knowing that the Light and Sound surrounds and protects us, and that the Living Master walks with us at all times.

How the individual's expansion of consciousness directly impacts Sugmad's Infinite Fabric

The flow of love through this universe has been constricted at times when the dark forces have been employed to reset the balance. In this new time, with the change of the frequencies in the Light and Sound that I have seen taking place, Sugmad's vibrancy has increased a hundred-fold. This comes only from the increased

21

Babaji

God-Realized energy of new souls seeking their way home to the heart of God. The revitalization of the spiritual waters that feed the cosmic matter of this universe has brought about a great change to this Sugmad. New levels of consciousness that were veiled by the Master have been revealed, because it is time for this universe to bring the new alignment of the God power into use and finally bring this cycle of grace and change to its new beginnings. The blending of other species from other Sugmads and universes; the transmutation of energy brought to us from other sources; the use of the dormant abilities of the greater Soul within each of us – all these things are at hand. The great effort to bring many to their rightful place as God-Realized souls in this Sugmad has long been awaited by us of the Ancient Orders from far beyond the boundaries of the Ocean of Love and Mercy. The call for a Living Master who is willing to take this journey with you was answered in Dan Rin, and with our blessing he has brought these new wonders that will exist in this Sugmad for time infinite. The universe is a melting pot of souls in continual manifestation.

How the individual makes the connection with the Light and Sound of God

Express the limitless love of God in all you do.

It is the ring within a ring within a ring, never seeming to touch, but forever connected. There is no need to make the connection to the Light and Sound for it to grow to the awareness of Soul's existence in the heart of God. We are never disconnected from the higher source of being; we only lose sight of it to enjoy the return to it. This is the limitless expression of Sugmad's awareness of Its love within Its love as the ring is within the ring. There is never seen the connection between the rings through mortal vision, but the unmistakable sense of the connection through the inner awareness of Soul is felt when the heart is opened when it is touched by the Divine Fire of God's everlasting love – the Light and Sound. It is the lapse in the memory of our beginnings,

22

brought on by the lower consciousness involvement in the worlds of duality that presents us with the illusion that we have been disconnected from God's love. So it is through selfless acts of love toward all in some small way that we can remind ourselves that we are connected to the heart of our Creator. It is with the simplest thought that we can open the communication with the heart of another and experience the joy of God's great gift to us all. The more this action guides us in our lives, the more of Sugmad's grace is presented to the lower worlds, and will bring about a greater alignment to the wishes of Sugmad. I have been here many times with you to bring this message again and again, in many different forms and practices, and it is now that the frequency of this love is more accessible to all, and more are being awakened in this great renaissance of the Light and Sound.

Why the seeker of God-Realization needs a spiritual teacher to reach the Sugmad's Ocean of Love and Mercy

When one is awakened to God's love, it is not so much a teacher that is to be sought, as it is the explanation for the change. The heart longs for the comfort of God's arms while the mental body tries to define existence through the limited understanding of ego. The true self awakens after its realization that there is more to the universe than its five senses; these are brought into alignment with the process of enlightenment which is the fuel for the fire of inner awareness of one's true self in the heart. This point on your journey may become somewhat complex. The energetic vibration of the God Worlds is very unusual to the newly God-Realized, and the help of the Masters on the inner and the assistance of the Living Master will aid Soul to acclimate to this new found frequency of love. You must learn to accept the heart-to-heart communication style in this realm of existence. A method to understand the language of this ancient wisdom will be provided to help accelerate your movement in these realms of beingness.

Babaji

How the seeker finds a spiritual teacher who is fitted to their spiritual goals

"When the student is ready, the teacher will appear".

The need to stay with the spiritual exercises to maintain an open and receptive heart is paramount at this time in your journey. From the inner guidance you will be put into the right trajectory to meet with the one to take you through this unfoldment with love and caring. The Way of Truth has been given for this task, and Dan Rin is best suited for this time to guide the quantity of souls that are approaching this level of awareness. This has been at the request of the Ancient Ones to bring new order to this universe at this time of its new beginnings.

The Beginning Has No End

A step-by-step contemplative exercise that will give the seeker an experience in the God Worlds

MISRADU-MISRADU-MISRADU-KU

This is an ancient mantra to open the heart to the vibratory understanding of the language of the Masters and all those who speak from the inner spiritual realms as to what direction we're moving in, and to offer us guidance. This allows the dialect of the Ancient Ones to be understood in the purest vibratory forms, but allows a useable translation for the mind to implement the methods given to accelerate your movement into the God Worlds. This is offered to those with the attitude of the pure, open, selfless transparent heart that seeks only to return home to the love of Sugmad.

Use the **HU** to center your consciousness in the sacred heart and to open the channel to the way of the Masters; use this mantra <u>three times</u> and sit in quiet contemplation to understand that which is beyond knowing.

Su lot tilnot tu dess tra dos tu dente neste' alt tente daspensé ot notē tel-lettis ma-ettas nus delmsi te.

This is a sample that was transmitted and left in its original dialect. (This spelling is the best that can be given.) It is a simple greeting to you who have chosen to walk in the higher realms of God Awareness. Repeat it the best you can and feel the change in your heart vibration.

Babaji

Chapter Three

Initiation

The initiation is the means for you to mark your stride and to help you maintain a pace that has been written into your universal contract as part of your karmic duties in this new order of the Sehaji that is being formed through The Way of Truth.

The Beginning Has No End

The nature and purpose of Initiation

When the seeker of the true knowledge of the Light and Sound requests passage into the many hidden temples, there must be a filter provided for the consciousness of the neophyte Soul in this new realm of experience. This is one of the first times that the process of initiation comes to bear on the experience of the journeying Soul in its usefulness and purpose. The initiations are deemed important by the Grand Council for the souls that are joining the God Worlds, and they are given to the Living Master to move people along this track of growth within. The Living Master is in touch with the needs and desires of the seeker and can see that its selflessness and its practice of the spiritual exercises have prepared it for the intensity of the understanding of these places of information that it has been drawn to on the road to Mastership. In this process the seeker becomes extremely grateful to all those involved with its ascent into God-Realization.

There is no numerical definition that truly describes a seeker's initiation level, for each Universal Soul Movement, in its own true understanding of what the Masters give at each juncture of unfoldment, cannot be compared to or analyzed by any mental qualitative process. It is the inner sight that allows the seeker to view the workings of the higher realms in complete understanding of his or her position in this journey. This is the grace of initiations; each one takes the seeker to a point of beginning. For the selfless heart Soul, traveling as a neophyte Master seeking its duty in Sugmad's order, this beginning has no end. The quality of the heart-to-heart transmissions that the initiate receives while in the wisdom temples and/or libraries is balanced by the vibration they experience as the Living Master watches over them. There is a replacement process that occurs at these times of learning given in the scrolls of wisdom that are available to you of the transparent sacred heart. The initiation is the means for you to mark your stride and to help you maintain a pace that has been written into your universal contract as part of your karmic duties in this new order of the Sehaji that is being formed through The Way of Truth. As you fulfill each portion of the growth that you feel within, all the knowledge and direction for each part of your new consciousness will be revealed in its proper order to provide the maximum benefit to this Sugmad and Its growth to spread love through the Light and Sound as It expands to touch more and more waiting souls, if they choose to accept the love of God in their hearts.

This is a template of understanding the function of initiation. The mental body can take and process the energy flow perceived as its own learning device. This energy flow is being fine-tuned so that you may share the vibration from this new frequency of Light and Sound carrying all back to the heart of Sugmad. Let not any idea that may have been placed in your consciousness beneath the veil of skepticism sway you from your purpose and duties in the karmic cycle of this universe, for there are those who would not have Dan Rin complete this great mission that you have joined with to bring a new balance and love to this Sugmad. Know that your initiation provides all this to you as it always has for those who have traveled before you and for those who will come after you.

What it means to be initiated into this life

Walking with the grace of God as your guide in this life requires the assistance of a spiritual Master to aid in your understanding the new energies that will be passing through your consciousness as you travel through the higher realms of beingness. To give each of you the most fulfilling experience, the Living Master of the Light and Sound is made aware of the frequencies of your spiritual duties in this Sugmad, and he offers an appropriate vibration to your inner body alignment so you can process the God flow that has become a part of you. The initiation is accompanied by a sacred word that is tuned precisely for you so that you may access the wisdom of the higher realms as you move along the path to God-Realization. The Master will come to you in your contemplations with knowledge that is to be given through you to those still unaware of

The Beginning Has No End

God's great love in this universe. Through you, its completion will be realized and this universe will be allowed to evolve to its next incarnation.

We are the tools that God uses to present Itself to those still lost in the mire of the worlds of duality and illusion. Through us, the sight of these lost souls may be opened to the grace of the love that brings each and every soul back to its true home in the heart of God. The initiation of this life is a great gift that each of us has been allowed to experience as we grow closer to our creator. Our closeness grows in every act of love that we perform through the selfless heart of a true seeker and in the highest frequencies of love and light. In this modality we send out the healing energy that is a part of the karmic duties of the initiates as they give themselves to the vibration of pure selflessness that comes from the heart when they each maintain a rigorous adherence to spiritual unfoldment through daily contemplation and acts of kindness. This healing energy is furthered through undying devotion to the guidance that is offered from all the Masters that have come to aid in this time of recalibration of the Light and Sound.

Coming to the aid of those that have been stalled by other paths, this new openness will greatly improve the flow of this newly calibrated love sent to heal the past karmic deeds that linger in this Sugmad from the misuse of the Light and Sound; that is to say, not letting it flow from a place of selfless love as occurred in other paths that have come before The Way of Truth. It has been my experience through the many lifetimes that I have spent guiding the wisdom of the highest laws of God to those that have shown themselves of a pure and selfless nature, that when misused it can cause a severe imbalance to the flow of energies that give the vibrancy of life to this and other universes. The minds of many have been drawn away from the true use of the gifts of Sugmad to profit for themselves and others that would use them. Initiations are a safeguard that can prevent this from happening, in that through these initiations, the Masters control the flow into the hearts of these souls seeking their path to the higher realms. When there is a sense that a heart is being clouded by the desire of the ego and the causal body, the flow to the initiate can be adjusted to bring them into better alignment with the wishes of Sugmad. These are the cases that appear from time to time when the level of vibration is too great for a particular Soul that has touched upon an area of consciousness prior to the unfoldment and opening of their true self.

The Light and Sound, when filtered by the mental body as ego, is clouded and can become unclear in its message of love. The mission at hand is one that requires the careful calibration through initiation of souls. The mission is threefold: to give this higher knowledge into the lower world, to draw the ever present grace of God to the awareness of all souls, and to bring a great state of oneness to the love that governs the progress of this universe in its journey back to God's heart. The many trials that have beset the travelers of the spiritual paths need to be showered with the light of selfless love and the vibrant sound of the purest knowledge that all souls belong in the heart of God.

How the initiation process differs in calibration of Light and Sound from initiations on the physical, astral causal, mental, and etheric planes

This is a discourse that should be well taught because of the tendency for many to be led astray by the familiarity of the vibration in the lower bodies and the tendency to consider them true transmissions of the Light and Sound. It's not to say that the Light and Sound do not infuse the love of God into every aspect of being; it is to say that the initiate should not assume that all knowledge is accessible to them through the lower bodies without the careful guidance of the inner Masters and the protection of the Living Master of the Light and Sound. The high vibration of the new Light and Sound can disrupt the pathways of logic, not unlike what occurs when an electrical surge blows out a light bulb, or when a sound frequency causes feedback over a loudspeaker system. Each initiation is specific to a level of awareness in each plane of existence: the physical, astral, causal, mental, etheric, and soul planes, and then finally stepping into true God Consciousness. The Light and Sound is carefully calibrated to bring the required wisdom that goes with unfoldment into the heart of the seeker, and the results that occur amongst those who seek God's love are as varied as the wildflowers of the fields. As the inner life of Soul begins to grow into its own awareness, the corresponding levels of the inner bodies go through their own evolution so that they may grow closer to the source of their creation. Each awareness that is within all of the lower bodies serves a purpose in the dispensing of the Light and Sound in the lower realms. Each must be calibrated by the Masters through the use of spiritual exercises, to attune it to its greatest use in the transmitting of love to all areas of life on the outer and inner journey. This is to bring the knowledge to the seekers that all of God's love is found in all of God's love.

Each avenue of unfoldment is just one more facet of light that shines the golden grace of Sugmad's glory into areas where this consciousness has never been offered before. This is the great task at hand and will be completed in this cycle of this Sugmad. The opening of the heavens is to let the true light of God's love shine in all the hearts of Its children still lost to the veiled illusion of the lower worlds, and to open every heart to the Light and Sound that carries the pure energy of selflessness that will show to those of lesser virtues that they also are a part of Sugmad's love. In the physical, the Light and Sound shows Itself in the joy that is seen in the eyes of a small child that can infect and change the mood of the most clouded heart. In the astral, the quality of the inner vision in the dream state is affected when the heart of the seeker feels the first vibration of its sacredness and ability to hear the Voice of God. There comes a time in every seeker's emotions that they experience "the heart cracking wide open". This may come after the Third or Fourth Initiation. It is the sense of an emotion of great magnitude filling the seeker's heart at some time when they realize that all the feelings that pass through this state of lower consciousness truly come from a higher source, and that this source has been calling to them for many lifetimes and has finally become irresistible.

The sudden clarity of mind as the level of Self-Realization draws near, is when the Light and Sound is calibrated by the Master to open the consciousness of the initiate to the possibilities beyond the self, and to let the first sight of God Consciousness filter through the ego to touch the opening heart of the initiate. This is a time in the life of the earnest seeker that the song of God's love is heard clearly for the first time, through the use of their sacred word and the HU. Mantras become much more potent as the heart's message becomes clearer to the third eye. As the seeker sees through the thin veil of the illusion, the Light and Sound has been known to break through with a brilliance that sometimes shocks the consciousness and may cause some to retreat from the process of unfoldment.

This is where some other paths have let the seeker fall into the slumber known as enlightenment and give the reward to the mental body for bringing the ego to this place of accomplishment. But those whose hearts have been opened through the astral and causal awareness of a higher source can see beyond the veil because of the complete integration of the Light and Sound at the new levels of access that have been brought into being through the efforts of the Sehaji Order, the Brakosani and the Living Master, Dan Rin. I have come to give this to you because, as I said, this is something that has not been shared for many Masterships, for only until now has there been a need for this great consciousness to bring Sugmad to Its greatest vibration in this beginning. Those of you who are Sixth and Seventh Level Masters have returned, and going through your Ninth Initiation of this cycle of Sugmad, will understand the need to increase the release of the Light and Sound at this raised frequency and to re-balance this universe and bring it back from the brink of annihilation. The constriction of the flow of spiritual energies has allowed the Lords of Darkness free reign over many souls for much too long, but they have now relented from their onslaught to allow that which is to come to have its beginning. The blessings that have been bestowed upon you as the new order of Sehaji are the greatest gift seen in many Sugmads. Carry well the knowledge that you are of the highest honored ones to usher in the greatest love to be seen in a millennium.

How the initiation directly affects the God seeker's expansion of consciousness

Once the heart has been opened during the journey home, it's difficult for the seeker to look at life with the same vision and understanding that they had been using in the lower vibrations of consciousness. As initiation begins the spiritual transformation and Soul becomes enlivened to the sound of God's voice growing ever closer to its consciousness, Soul will always respond as long as the heart is truly selfless and open to the energy of the Divine Love that the Masters present through the initiation process. The initiate understands the glory that is found in the love from the heart of Sugmad, and will carry the mercy and love of God across the Great Divide back to the waiting souls that slumber. The initiate, having this duty to perform, begins to broaden as Soul. This expansion in consciousness is the result of the seeker's devotion to the calling of the Sehaji to their Mastership role. The one thing that the seeker who has given himself to the guidance of the Living Master realizes is the need to follow the beckoning of the Master's subtle direction. The lessons that are laid before the initiate can involve the Soul in a journey to a new place to see if it can maintain the levels of the Light and Sound. If so, it will bring the Light and Sound to those that wait for an inner awakening so they may embark on the same journey as the initiate. This is the special gift that you of The Way of Truth have been afforded by the Sehaji, for Dan Rin has taken care in bringing only those of the highest aspiration toward living in the God Realized state to his side, and protects this group with the love that only he has been privy to in the last 2,000 years in this Sugmad. To revitalize the Children of Africa and to bring balance back to this Sugmad, the expansion of the consciousnesses of the Initiates of The Way of Truth was accelerated to provide the opening necessary for the energies of Ekere Tere to flow through to the willing seekers who dedicate themselves to the way of God-Realization.

To accomplish this within the current cycle, it was necessary to bring the tremendous love of God's heart to the Light and Sound. This caused a rise in vibration of the love in these seekers of selfless being to reach the God Worlds and to provide the blessing for those below the Great Divide who have yet to reach this new consciousness. This Sugmad has longed for the completion of Its desire to spread love to those that still slumber in the illusions of the mind and causal planes, and who choose to suffer rather than rejoice in the growth that the passing karmic energies have left behind. As we have lifted Dan Rin to the level of a Sixth Master at the 17th Initiation Level, this universe is now poised to release the greatest love infusion to the cosmos that has ever been requested by any Sugmad. When your initiations have lifted you to the prescribed frequencies, you will be able to see that your future karmic duties, as Sehaji Masters, are those of being sent on Universal Soul Movement to many other universes and Sugmads to teach and guide other great souls that have suffered through this constriction of Light and Sound in their evolutions, and are awaiting blessings sent by this Sugmad through you. You are the great wonder that only the everlasting love from the heart of creation can foster, and you shall succeed where others have failed.

What determines the gift of an initiation upon the God seeker

This is not the first time for many of you in this position; I do remember you from times before as I have offered many other Masters that which you have accepted in initiations along with this mission. The rapid initiation cycle that you have just emerged from, was granted by the Grand Council, the Silent Nine, Kal

The Beginning Has No End

Niranjan, and the Red Dragon Order. The Lords of Karma were taken in to counsel at the request of Dan Rin, and were given the order to reduce the karmic activity so that you could proceed unencumbered by the cycles of karmic retribution that many souls travel through as they aspire to the doorway of the God Worlds. The reason for this was to prepare a group for the needs of this Sugmad. The greatest gift that has ever been given was bestowed upon those of The Way of Truth, for as I have said, you have been observed through other lifetimes and Masterships, and it is felt that you are now ready to be released from the cycles of karmic battles.

A seeker of the God Worlds is seen from above as a Soul of great capacity to love and understand those of ignorance that are caught in the illusion of suffering and pain. Souls that have let themselves be seduced by the mental body into believing that the consciousness of Self-Realization is the highest aspiration in this Sugmad have been led asunder by their spiritual leaders – those that have used the Light and Sound for their own egoistic gains of power and wealth. This is why this Sugmad has sought you out to bring the new higher frequencies of Light and Sound into operation, to restore balance and to release those ready to move once again towards the heart of God. As this takes place, you will be allowed to see the actual change in the vibration of those hearts that have been closed to you before. As you continue your growth, you will be shown the energetic talents and mantras that will be used to give these souls a path to their new initiatory processes. We have all, at times in our incarnations, been blinded by the will of the lower bodies. We have also been gifted with the open-hearted consciousness that has brought us back each time with knowledge that primed us for the levels of initiation deemed necessary to us by the spiritual hierarchy of this universe. I say "we" because even though I have ascended to the highest levels of awareness in my Mastership, I could only accomplish this by existing in all forms of consciousness and transmuting the vibration of those planes into the wisdom that I have passed on to all those that have come after me since time immemorial.

Use well this great gift that the Ancient Ones have allowed to be granted to you. Let your selfless, sacred heart continue to open to the love of Sugmad.

How initiation affects the spiritual signature of Soul

You may ask how we know of your merits, for there are truly an infinite number of journeyers traveling to and through the higher realms of consciousness. Each of these precious beings are of great importance to God and all have a very distinct place in the vast Ocean of Love and Mercy where we commune in the love of God's heart. You, a seeker of God-Consciousness, have been singled out and given special vibratory signatures that the Masters can access when you visit on the inner to seek their counsel and guidance. As you take the frequency of your initiation and continue to move it and yourself as Soul closer to the heart of God, you become recognized by the guardians of the wisdom temples by this vibration. As you ascend, the change in your spiritual identity allows the hierarchy to prepare the mantle of wisdom that you will wear when you have been trained and are ready to return as Masters to aid those in the lower worlds on their spiritual journeys. Remember, an initiation is merely the process of gaining the permission, which is granted by the Masters, to grow into your true and complete self. You, as Soul, must take all that is stored within your lifetimes of learning and karmic contract and apply it to your journey. It is the energy that helps power the light that illuminates your path to the God Worlds. The stronger your stride, the brighter the light will shine.

Why the level of initiation correlates with the spiritual freedom of Soul

The seamless effort to pass from one initiation to the next comes through the practice of your spiritual exercises, for they have the purpose of aligning the lower consciousness of the lower worlds to be more in tune with the progress that you make as Soul. The greater the Light and Sound in your practices, the further you travel on the Inner with each touch of God's love to your open selfless heart. The understanding of the wisdom temples that you visit will become easier to blend into the lower consciousness of the daily life that you lead. When Soul becomes attuned to its ability to take the Light and Sound everywhere in its existence, the physical, astral, causal, and mental bodies work as sign posts in the etheric for Soul to access passage to the God Realms when journeying to the cities on the higher planes. The spiritual freedom for seekers to share with those they encounter in all realms is increased. The heart-to-heart exchange that takes place on the Inner will gain more clarity with less dependency upon mantras to tune the consciousness when in conversation with the Keepers of Wisdom and Knowledge that inhabit the great cities of the higher realms. We wish only for you to gain access to the God energy that has been placed within you to bring joy to all who commune together in the Ocean of Love and Mercy.

How initiation took me into a deeper understanding of life

I have traveled between the beginning and the transition of time itself into eternity, and have not yet completed all the initiate duties that have been granted to me. Over the eons of my presence in God's eyes, I have taken the movement of my consciousness to many universes with great joy, and have been involved with many different species and manifestations of beingness throughout Sugmad after Sugmad. The greatest awareness I have gathered is that love is the language by which all beings communicate. Even though in other dialects the sound and description of this energy may seem different, the exchange is unmistakable. This is what I have continued to bring back to the consciousness of those who reside in every form of existence. I have shown myself in corporeal form to only a few, but have given the love in my soul to all that sought me out in every effort to learn the secrets of sharing the great love of God. For those that wish to journey with me, know in the innermost part of your selfless heart that I am that which is there to guide you on your quest. As can be heard in the words that I have shared with others of your desire, the simplest acts of love will bring the greatest result to every experience on all planes of consciousness. Know that my journeys have taken me to all planes of awareness. If you wish, I can be found in your dreams on the astral. The love that I have gained from Sugmad Itself can be felt in the causal with all the exchanges of the emotional heart. I have lit the fire of inquiry in your mental body as it comes closer to the acquisition of the God Consciousness in Soul as you travel on the etheric. Know that I stand next to Dan Rin when you give yourself completely to Soul, your true existence in the heart of God. Sing the glorious songs of love, and journey to wondrous visions on the inner planes of knowingness and beingness. All awareness is the expression of life, and to live is to experience the love in the heart of Sugmad.

Some experiences I had in my initiatory trek to God-Realization

There was the time when I was called to return in a human form to the spiritual Masters of the time to notify them of the need for all humankind to learn to care for each other and to share the bounty of this physical existence. The lesson to teach was one that brought an inner initiation, and it brought one of the greatest visions that my heart had ever experienced – a vision of the future where all souls and the Light and Sound were merged and the greatness of God's love was actually visible in your universe, and shining more brightly than any celestial body in the sky of your galaxy. This was a moment that was imprinted in all my teachings from that moment on, and I feel that it had to be the reason that so many seek my council and guidance on so many different questions of being. You will see in this cycle through the eyes of your soul, the epoch of the true beginning of selfless love between all people of your planet. This is in preparation for the arrival of those that planted seeds of existence of the human kind from which you, as souls, have evolved. The blending of your genetic and spiritual DNA will open the vortex that lies just out of sight of your energy spectrum. This vortex houses the communication of the change in the Light and Sound activated by your spiritual renaissances. Be well aware that this is the true manifestation of God's love in this universe and the complete understanding of the Light and Sound is in your heart as I speak to you. Know that the love Sugmad has for you is greater than any yet expressed in my journeys across time itself.

How reincarnation relates to initiation and the spiritual development of the God seeker

One of the simplest ways to learn is by repetition; reincarnation is repetition of action as the consciousness is slowly awakened to the presence of God in all things. Through all levels of awareness, the Soul is gradually groomed for its emergence into complete consciousness of itself and its duties to Sugmad's love. The rare qualities of the initiation that have been granted by the Grand Council in this cycle show that there is a compassion in the hierarchies for the care of all the souls that are a part of this Sugmad's health. Some of you may realize that you have been relieved of certain karmic exercises in your last life cycle. The lessons that are presented during reincarnation cycles are those that need to be imprinted in the hearts of those that have the greatest duties pending in their soul contracts. As I have shared in my own experiences, the things that you may be chosen for are usually things of great importance to Sugmad, so learn well from your dreams; you will revisit past lives there. Remember, they are subtle reminders that are left in your consciousness to take along on this round of God-Realization that you have chosen.

How the initiatory processes breaks the reincarnation cycle of the Wheel of the 84 for Soul

Once awareness has been brought to the etheric level and Soul stands awake, the initiatory process can take on a different meaning for the God seeker. The true, transparent, selfless heart must be aspired to through rigorous spiritual exercise. The heart must remain open to the language of the Masters to better understand the need for complete cooperation with the Lords of Karma who govern the Wheel of 84. It is only they, at the Master's request, who step forward to relieve you of this burden because of your importance to this Sugmad. As Dan Rin has often explained, for the first time in this and any other Sugmad, there is an agreement with all levels of the hierarchy above and below the Great Divide to bring into existence a new level of the Light and Sound - one that reaches all souls in this universe so that the balance of the spiritual realms can never be disturbed again. This is the greatest mission ever embarked upon by a chosen group, and you have been chosen for Mastership within the cycle of the present Sehaji Master.

The Beginning Has No End

A Step-by-step contemplative exercise with a mantra that will develop more love and understanding for life

We have traveled outside this universe to bring back to you this powerful exercise to create an engram with your selfless heart that will grow in its intensity with each subsequent initiation. This will tune your ability to love with that of Sugmad; it gives you a clear vision of what to do to bring the true essence of the Light and Sound into every action of being, and how to do it. It will carry with it the information from another race of beings who have studied our evolution of love and wish to lend their findings to the re-awakening of love in all souls as they prepare to join with us once again.

As always, clear your mind of thoughts with <u>five</u> **HU**'s and center your attention on opening the heart through the third eye consciousness.

The words QUA-SALTU will open the vortex.

Then <u>repeat three times each</u> of these words in three syllables:

TE-NE-SIA

TE-NO-SIA

TE-NA-SIA

This is based on the tetrahedron design from Gopal Das.

Babaji

The nature and meaning of consciousness

Consciousness is the light that shines on the darkness of our ignorance to the love that is present in Sugmad's heart for us to share. All that is given to us in our search for our true self in Soul causes this light to shine ever more brightly in the night through which Soul wanders lost and yet to be awakened. The need for each open heart to reach out to any Soul in passing is how we will fill this Sugmad once again with all of Its joy. The acts of love that exist in balance with the change and growth of the karmic processes will aid in the spread of knowledge to other ways of life that still labor under the illusion of power and control. This, when referred to as "the necessary evil", is just the acknowledgement that this universe is alive with the Light and Sound and is the true expression of God's love for Itself manifested in all souls. Consciousness is also the light that shines through to the lower awareness of the lower bodies as they are the vehicles that bring great joy to each of you as you discover the existence of Soul, even in this grosser form of exchange in the physical realm.

This provides us with the opportunity to reach out in acts of love that ring the harmonics of heaven to all that sleep in this illusion. The Lords of lower realms maintain the illusion as lessons in order to insure that when we enter into the ascent toward the God Worlds, we understand that it is through God's desire for us to experience Its love. Consciousness is truly that great light of warmth that we step into when we see through our selfless, sacred heart center into the future that will bring us to the Ocean of Love and Mercy. Bring with you the songs of praise that reverberate the highest energy of the Light and Sound and Truth of God's love for all things in existence. Consciousness is not a factor of the mind or for mental debate, but a great gift on the inner that allows the adventure of discovery of your true selves in love and light through compassion and a devotion to caring for others.

The Beginning Has No End

How we can align our consciousness with the Sugmad on a moment-to-moment basis

To balance this Sugmad, it has been taught that only true acts of selfless love bring the joy that fills Its heart. To look at our actions through the eyes of Soul rather than that of ego and selfish pride, brings a higher vibration of devotion to caring for one another to our daily lives; that is, not to ask what it is that we need today, but what it is that we can give today through the selfless love that is bestowed so freely to each of us. The reason for the journey is to share the discovery of love and to show us at all times that this life is truly a gift that must be shared in all expressions of thoughtfulness towards those that we encounter still wandering in the illusion of pain and suffering; and therefore, to truly understand that God is the energy that drives every aspect of the Light and Sound seen through the eyes of the open heart in all beings encountered in this limited environment we call the physical. Our everyday duty to Sugmad is to share the knowledge of the heart and to show, through selfless acts of caring, the awareness that everyone is a part of the Light and Sound in this universe. You may travel on the inner with the knowledge that, through your spiritual practices, all is granted to you from those planes of existence that you are privy to. Let the message of Self-Realization in Soul lead to the God energy manifesting in this day-to-day life.

Caring for one another is the grace of the true Soul that has aligned itself with Sugmad, again and again, throughout each day. It is the nourishment for this universe as it begins to open to its new beginning. Let the Light and Sound be felt in the simplest exchange of greeting. Let the heart of God be your only guide when you come to a crossroad of feelings. Let the light of your God Self shine on those moments of indecision that cause confusion on the causal and emotional planes, and always know that the Living Master of the Light and Sound watches over the outcome of all dilemmas you may face. Let your heart be touched by the hearts of others that have sought what you exchange with the Sugmad in your contemplations, so that they may find their way to the planes of true joy and love.

Remember it is the simple attitude of love that makes the greatest change in the outcomes of your day.

How consciousness plays a key factor in the compatibility of the male-female relationship

If love is the true exchange of wisdom, then that which is infused in consciousness will be exchanged in matters of the heart between two people who care for each other. The light that fills your hearts is what should be given when we express our caring of one to another. As the levels of consciousness are raised through seeking the God within us, the rate and exchange of inter-personal relationships will gain the clarity and purity of the Light and Sound and begin to grow into a combined heart that shows its praise to Sugmad when these two hearts share their love for each other. To have this gift in your consciousness broadens the path through which love can pass. The only outcome that would be seen is that of the presence of a greater love of God that this love between you shows. Once again I come back to the idea of simplicity of desire and action. The selfless open heart is the key to resolution when hearts fail to meet on common ground. Stop for the moment and let yourselves reconnect to that which has given this experience of love to you, and once again remember that you are Soul sharing God's love throughout this universe, and only that consciousness can bring the alignment of the perfect expression of love that is a part of the selfless heart of the God seeker. When our God Awareness is expressed in our day-to-day relations, all who have the gift of this awareness of the high source of being will travel through this temporal representation of God's love with ease and grace. A part of the mission in this Sugmad is to bring the new vibration of the Light and Sound closer to the exchanges in the lower realms of existence. This occurs through the effort to express this in your relationships with a passion that expresses the need for a constant contact with our higher self in Soul. The physical intimacy of the expression of God's love is where the true consciousness of the presence of God is felt in the exchange of love.

How we can achieve the highest degree of Godliness in our relationship with our beloved

When you are in this world of the physical, you must at all times bring the openness of your true self to every moment. When you can find the presence of the God power in those day-to-day relationships outside of those with your heart mates, the richness of those experiences brings a heightened awareness to that which you share with your beloved. Know in yourself that the blending of two souls of the true, selfless heart will bring about a new and vibrant understanding of the deeper, inner workings of your relationship with the one you love most intimately. The Light and Sound fills your every action if the heart is centered in the grace that is presented to us in each day of our lives. The step-by-step change in your soul awareness will manifest in all those things that are closest to your heart, for that which you experience in the higher realms of the inner will be yours in all your daily expressions of love to your beloved. Always express God's love in your touch. In the center of your beingness there can only be that which is best suited for the growth of Soul as a true seeker of the God realms, so you must find this center in the sight of your heart as you look to the highest aspect of your beloved. The nectar of the flower of passion will forever be present in this love that is graced by the highest vibration of your God Self.

How the individual consciousness is affected and influenced by Universal Consciousness

We where born from a single prospect of being, then shattered into experiences and beingness with a purpose to once again be joined with our beginning. In each of us is the desire to know of that which has created this, and as we journey through all levels of awareness we slowly gain within our being the sense that we have been placed here for a simple but illusive reason. When the first hint of God's love was felt in the earliest awakening of Sugmad, the die was cast as to the process of Soul's journey. The overall feeling that spread throughout the universe was one of mystery as to why all seemed a part of everything, yet appeared separate in many realms of consciousness. This was instilled into what is now called Soul, but was in its beginning the flash of existence coming into being, and has ever since been in the process of returning to Itself and bringing great joy to Itself. We know not of whence we came, but all that we wish is to be one with our beginning again. This is the Universal Consciousness that floods the sea of cosmic vibrations that have been set in motion by what we now describe as Sugmad, and Its action of awareness of Itself is the love that we are all part of and seek to experience in the highest possible realms of understanding. As we evolved into Soul we were given an opening into the light called consciousness which shines into the darkness called discovery. We are set in action to bring this light to all areas of being that we have become aware of. As we, in our individual expression of this great experience grow, so does this consciousness called Sugmad reach for Itself to once again embrace us all as Itself. I return to the simplest ideas, because within this is the key to greater understanding. We must care for one another with all the love that has been given to use by the divine energy of this universe in God's heart.

The role of family in our development as Soul and how this relates to our soul contract in this life

Looking back across the Great Divide from within, as Soul is raised to the God Worlds, we see the tentacles of karmic connection to those close to us in our families. Understanding of these connections is best given through Universal Soul Movement via a request to the Masters that will allow you to view the karmic scrolls. But it is no mistake that how we progress along the journey

The Beginning Has No End

to God-Realization has an immense effect on those closest to us on the karmic rungs of evolution. Bringing the God energy into your everyday life is best seen in the reflection of those souls that link to you through the process of family. Each contract that has been built for later review as the family progresses, is to establish a strong and more permanent flow of love from Sugmad to all those that are coming into this new awareness of the presence of the Light and Sound in the lower realms of consciousness. When each member of this karmic circle called family is presented with its time to move closer to Soul's awakening, the contracts are once again reviewed upon request of the leading Master involved. As all aspire to bring the love of this Sugmad to Its highest vibration, the strength of the family connection will greatly increase as will the drive towards the selflessness that is required to allow the love of the Creator to shine through to illuminate that path which is laid before all that seek the divine in one another.

The reach for the God Worlds is one that each and every Soul has the right to experience; however, the freewill that is granted by overseers of the lower planes can cloud the judgment of some. However, if someone in a family has a serious contract that needs to be brought before the Council to aid in this Sugmad's rediscovery of Its true balance, then it becomes a matter that is handled through the exchange of other members of the karmic string, and is brought to the attention of the Red Dragon Order as to how to move this Soul back into its true trajectory towards the God Worlds. I have offered this to you so that you will know that there is a complexity to the growth of each individual Soul as it is linked with all those that are of the same karmic signature called family that may cross many lifetimes. But in this time of this beginning, all aspects of the universal laws are available for change if so deemed by the spiritual hierarchy of this Sugmad.

Babaji

Describe the training of Dan Rin and how you worked as a liaison for him and Milati in the Sehaji's best-laid plans to balance Sugmad's universe

When the name Dan Rin was presented to the Grand Council, it took awhile for the laughter to subside.

Milati stepped forward and presented to the Council a scroll of great volume which he and I had compiled of Dan Rin's growth and experiences in the Light and Sound over many lifetimes. The moment when he reached the 2nd Level of Mastership, he was not ready to accept the initiations that went with its responsibilities, and he was returned to a more severe karmic cycle to gain the understanding that he would be given a much higher Mastership whether or not he was ready. Then when he was returned as a 6th Level Master and given this mission of The Way of Truth he readily accepted the new levels of Initiation that had been prepared by the Silent Ones, for they had known from time beyond time that this Great Soul would be able to pilot the sea of turmoil and resistance that lay ahead of him in his training. To take a soul and move it quickly from a 7th Level Master to the 17th Level Initiation, and then to ask him to re-balance this Sugmad and create a new frequency of love in the Light and Sound, and further to find souls of great merit to join us in the new shape of this Sugmad, the Council saw in him the same that we had as we watched him grow in his capacity for the transparent selfless beingness. He could transmit the intense levels of the God power frequencies necessary to bring about the change that was happening. We are blessed by this Sugmad for bringing this Great Soul into this universe to once again perform the miracle of spreading the message of the great love of Sugmad. Once Dan Rin's mission was activated, the Sehaji Order revealed itself. At the same time those of the former conduit of the Light and Sound, the Varja Order, set in place the necessary constraints to maintain the universal spiritual balance to allow the opening of Ekere Tere in order to release the power of the suppressed souls of Africa and bring forth this time of renaissance in the heart of Sugmad. It was a time of joy when the Mantle of the Rod of Power was placed upon him and the glory of Sugmad's heart increased a thousand fold because It knew of the virtues and compassion of this chosen Master. Know that, as the true Living Master of the Light and Sound, he will guide you as we all bring this awareness to souls that have waited for this time of beginnings. Blessed with the ancient arts of prophecy and Universal Soul Movement, he has gathered the threads of the mysteries left to us by Christ, Mohammed, Krishna, Buddha and many other past Masters of the Light and Sound, for this time of teaching and mentoring the numbers of souls requested to perform this miracle of love and devotion to God would not be a simple task. With the assistance of the Sehaji Order and over 300 other Masters, this universe has been placed in the hands of a divinely groomed Being.

How religion and other life-paths have their own field of consciousness and how this affects the soul's development of life-understanding

The Light and Sound is forever present in all efforts to be aligned with the will of Sugmad. When the need arises for a guide for souls wandering in illusion, there are those of limited consciousnesses who have attained a level of Self-Realization and have only had a hint of that which lies just beyond that level of awareness. They have set out to offer those still lost what they themselves have barely touched. This consciousness of limited experience, not completely infused with ageless wisdom carried in the Light and Sound, can bring a sense of the love of God to only the minds of those seeking the comfort of knowing great love in this universe. What is lacking is the continuous fire to be consumed in this love – a love that forever brings joy and wonderment to the Soul that truly seeks to lose itself in the Divine Love of Sugmad. When the belief is held that the illusion of love is seen in the gains of material manifestation of a great presence, a constriction in the flow of Light and Sound begins and the end result is stagnation to the souls that are held in this illusion. This is why the Light and Sound will shift and change frequencies to continue to present the love of Sugmad to all that come forward to join other selfless seekers who only want the best for humanity. The vision of those that choose to constrict the flow is soon taken away and the fire that once may have burned in that way of life will only flicker. As The Way of Truth becomes the beacon of the Light and Sound, all that have been touched by it before will once again be revitalized, for in Dan Rin the gates of heaven have once again been opened to all the waiting souls that wander in the lower worlds of duality and illusion. I have spent much time with this One and know his compassion for those that have been misled; his desire is only to give to whoever steps forward and requests to be guided to the love of Sugmad once again.

The Beginning Has No End

A step-by-step contemplative exercise that will open the consciousness of the seeker to the beauty of the moment in everyday life

The simplest way to understand the joy of love in life today is to be present. In your morning contemplation request that you be focused through the selfless heart awareness of Soul as you walk through your day. Always show caring for those you encounter in your daily travels and know in your heart that you are a messenger of Sugmad's love for all souls.

After <u>five</u> **HU's**, say inwardly three times:

I am the embodiment of the highest laws of Sugmad.

You may re-charge this energy any time during the day by simply repeating it inwardly.

Babaji

Chapter Four

The Lessons in Life

Truth, a frequency of love, is forever present in the eye of the selfless heart.

The Beginning Has No End

How the lessons in life give Soul's existence meaning and value

Life is full when you allow the God being within you to influence all that you undertake each day. Living within the mortal shell presents many opportunities to experience the joy of the Light and Sound in the simple ways of manifestation. As you move through this realm of actualization, the chance to operate from the higher planes of awareness within you will bring the Light and Sound closer to the purpose for which Sugmad has changed Its frequencies. Day-to-day living is the process of abandoning the lower consciousness's desires and needs to influence your actions and to embrace the heart as guide. The need to feel that everything in life is directed by a mix of karma and ego denies the higher self the ability to share the God essence. Soul has the ability to reach from within and provide guidance in many basic life activities. The touch of the Light and Sound is what enriches the emotional exchanges that take place between people every day. The great change in you is the knowledge that the God essence in you is your origin of operation. This strengthens Soul's presence in our moment-to-moment interplay in the lower realms of expression.

Remember that God's love exists everywhere in this universe on the inner and the outer. It is the wish of Sugmad that Its consciousness be shared in this way, and you, as an Initiate of the Light and Sound, have the inherent duty in your soul contract to touch those souls that you encounter that may still be locked in the beliefs of other ways of life that have taken away their spiritual freedom. The strength of Soul is increased by your daily dependence on Sugmad to bring you guidance in moments of confusion, doubt and fear. All is within the range of Sugmad's love and presence. I have said many times throughout this exchange that the simplest act of caring brings the greatest focus of love through you. As you begin to use the God power through the process of the selfless open heart, Soul gains more of an understanding about what it's like to operate from the God

Consciousness within. Every process of life is one more act of love toward realizing the presence of Sugmad.

What we can learn in life by keeping our attention on God

My experience when in the corporeal form has been that living in the physical world is a challenge that can only be met with complete focus on the God power within. I have seen in my disciples a marked change of consciousness when they have followed the exercises that were given and spent sufficient time in contemplation daily, always remembering to walk in the God Consciousness of their being. Passing through the interchange in living with all levels of awareness teaches the seeker of God to recognize Soul in all its forms. To move past judgment and uncertainty when encountered by other beings manifested in the physical is one of the lessons that the Masters may present to you. What is seen on the inner as you become more attuned will be of value to you in this life that you lead on the outer. I am speaking directly to the lower aspects of your being to bring them to the understanding that all things transpire from the heart of God. Some aspects of this part of Soul's journey may cause the necessity to travel with the lower emotions and to experience the pains of the human condition, but these things require the Initiate to bring from within the knowledge that all is a part of the love growing in your heart. Do not ask why to these things. Always take a moment of contemplation when the mind begins to offer its conclusions and refocus on the answer that Soul provides from the guidance that you receive from all those Masters that walk with you. To know what you must grow away from, you must pass through that which creates you – life.

How we can share the love and joy of living without intruding upon the spiritual space of others

You should know that the Light and Sound emanates from the transparent selfless heart of the true seeker, and the joy that is carried in that vibration will be shared with all you encounter. Even the most closed heart will feel the joy that is present in you when you walk in the God mind within yourself. The energy is never intrusive because it is the manifested joy of Sugmad that is being offered. All beings have the capacity to love in varying stages of development and levels of awareness; the harmonies that this creates are those of love being exchanged. I have found that even the most unconscious heart is still vulnerable to the effects of a loving consciousness. Spiritual development in Soul is well ready to receive love when it is offered in the purest form – that is, from our higher source of being. Initiates of The Way of Truth, you have been guided by Dan Rin to live your lives in the consciousness of love through the God-Realized state of awareness. If a Soul is encountered that is locked in a negative karmic cycle, even it will respond to the touch of Sugmad manifesting through your selfless nature. For after all, you have been offered the chance to be the messengers of this great awareness that is filling this universe.

Why Soul must gain its liberation through living life in a physical shell

The highest vibration of the causal body is its ability to be creative. As the awareness of Soul grows in all the lower bodies, it brings the emergence of this true self closer to the true manifestation of cosmic love directly from the Heart of God. Soul will change all levels of vibration as it carries the Light and Sound into every molecule of existence. Soul learns to express its essence, the love of Sugmad, in many ways creatively through the mortal shell that carries it to the pinnacle of wisdom in the lower realms of awareness; this process is well learned by those who would be Masters in their own right, as the Sehaji have promised to you, the true seekers. This coarse tissue that surrounds us in the physical shell has within it the presence of the Light and Sound, and even though its vibration is much lower than that of pure Soul, it is still a harmonic of that love that is the God power. As the Light and Sound is drawn across the Great Divide to the causal Plane, the highest vibration will be activated and the wonders of expression that manifest can truly be called art. Hearts of the purest desire have been able to produce some of the greatest efforts of manifesting this level of love through many modalities and expressions of the lower self that are still present in many art museums around the globe. I must, at some time, bring more light into the understanding that all souls have this great ability. It is only to clear the mind of its preconceived attitudes that prevent all from understanding this aspect of Soul's need to be liberated from the seeming bond of the physical shell. Remember, we deal with a world of illusion and dualities.

How the God seeker discerns what truth is in what is read, heard, and learned

Truth, a frequency of love, is forever present in the eye of the selfless heart. It shines brightly as to be found even when it is veiled by those of lesser virtue. Every mode of communication carries this vibration of truth, and when we have attuned ourselves to the love of God, it will resonate when we encounter it in speech, writing and prophecy. Truth cannot be hidden from the selfless sacred heart of the God seeker. Its vibration is one that is well learned as we have traveled through the lower realms of duality and illusion. This universe is comprised of the great truth of love in many forms, and as we open ourselves to the complete love of Sugmad, we respond to truth when we experience the consciousness of God within us. My experience is shared with you in these exchanges as truth that I have brought back from across existence itself.

Why the heart must take a leading role in what we acquire as knowledge

We have been speaking of truth, and the heart is that which resonates readily when it encounters this level of love called truth. All knowledge is infused with truth and when we seek guidance in the knowledge of those that passed before, it is the heart that we search with, for if we have purified it in the love of Sugmad, it will always take to the highest vibration of all communications. You need to rely upon the heart as the focal point of guidance, because it is attuned to the subtlest sound of God's voice in all things across all realms. The likelihood of illusion masquerading as truth is only possible if one has closed the heart to Soul's desire for the fire of truth in God's love. Whatever you come to as truth will only pass through the most open transparent heart, for it is truly in harmony with the pure essence of Sugmad.

What we ultimately learn in this life that fully captures God's infinite creative purpose

This life is not about caring for what we can or cannot do, but is about the love that is carried by the Light and Sound to all souls that wait for the awakening to Sugmad's love in their lives. The great act of compassion is to listen to the Soul that is still searching for its liberation from illusion, to understand deep within yourself the need to bring this compassion to all those who still linger in suffering and those who stand in hesitation, and to awaken them with the touch of Sugmad's love that you carry in the God-Consciousness of the selfless heart. You are the messengers of the Light and Sound in manifestation. This is what the Sehaji have infused in you and are leading you to use in every aspect of beingness. Yours is the joy that this Sugmad has been waiting for since the beginning that has no end.

Babaji

A contemplative exercise to expand and widen the seeker's awareness of life's gems of knowledge

Within each of your lives there are treasures yet unfound of the great gifts with which you have been blessed. Let me come to you and guide you to these wonders that may still be hidden from your awareness.

Sit in quiet contemplation with a focus on the opening of the heart. Say the mantra, **PARA TA HAR BRAHMAN** five times. Then call to me, Babaji, three times.

When you feel my presence, we shall say this mantra together for 5 to 10 minutes.

As the knowledge of these things may be unknown to you, use this technique three days and your inner vision will be focused on these things that we will find together.

What will be revealed to you will happen over the next two weeks after we have spent this time together. You will find them in some place and experience where you least expect to.

Chapter Five

Changing the Focus to Soul

Soul operates from a position of selfless nature and aspires to care for this Sugmad and Its wish to fill all hearts with Its love.

The Beginning Has No End

Why the emphasis should always be on the Soul aspect of others

We have a great connection to one another through our higher aspects of being – that of Soul. The communication from Sugmad to the many seekers on their return to Its heart is easily won through the effort of staying focused on the true self in Soul. As the Light and Sound is best conveyed from the higher realms through the vehicle of Soul, it is imperative that the consciousness be focused on the inner center of beingness, the heart, that which speaks to Soul directly and is the connection between the outer experience of life and the inner reality of life's purpose. The soul energy that is the essence of our God Self needs the nourishment of the selfless love that is exchanged between Sugmad and those who seek Its presence in all that they experience. This quality of life brings a sense of connection to a great process in this universe, namely, the achievement of the karmic work that has been set forth in this Sugmad.

This work of glorious love brings the universe into balance and provides the healing that has been long awaited by many who have yet been awakened to it. The steps that are being taken to bring the Light and Sound closer to the hearts of these souls and to awaken the soul energy in all that remain locked in the cycle of the Wheel of 84 have been well planned. In this Sugmad is realized the need to bring a balance directed by a love that is of such a high frequency that it will reverse the damage caused by the domination of the Lords of Darkness that have been a part of this awakening. Those that will be brought into the consciousness of Soul once again will be from all ways of life, philosophies, religions and spiritual doctrines that have lost touch with the true essence of beingness – the Light and Sound that brings God's love to all reality. As we communicate soul to soul, the transformation of these earthly journeys is enriched with the presence of the infinite love of Sugmad in all that you do for one another through acts of the selfless heart. Soul operates from a position of selfless nature and aspires to care for this Sugmad and Its wish to fill all hearts with Its love. To be awakened brings the hope and joy that you have been granted in seeking to be brought back to your true selves in Soul. God's love is a great energy that will fill you when the open selfless heart is engaged in the process of "giving and receiving" and caring with detached goodwill towards all.

Why and how karma is incurred whenever our attention is taken off of Soul consciousness

As you live through the journey of soul from within the mortal shell and the trials you endure to gain the riches of discovering your true self as Soul, you may stumble when the lower consciousness engrams of fear, doubt, anger, hate and lost contact with the love that fills your true heart, shows itself. This is when you have lost inner alignment with Soul. This is where Kal Niranjan and the Lords of Karma are very exacting about their duties to maintain the cosmic balance that allows the Light and Sound to move through this universe. You will find that in the lower aspects of being you may be thrown back to re-experience the emotions that brought about the lack of a soul connection to heart. This reactivates these old engrams and possibly blocks your connection to the selfless love of Sugmad ever present in you, when you focus on caring for one another in your daily lives.

When this imbalance is manifested in action, the karmic scrolls are adjusted and a life experience of equal or greater energy is established to bring the balance of your particular duties in this Sugmad back in order. The requirement of an act of greater compassion is usually the indicator that this imbalance has occurred. If you have established an awareness of the God power in the selfless Soul, and you travel through a vortex that casts you back to a less-than-loving way of being, you know that this is part of the process in your journey, and is meant to strengthen your abilities when you encounter less-than-caring forces. These forces can be countered by the energetic protection provided by the

The Beginning Has No End

Living Master when you strive to completely replace non-conscious beingness with God Knowingness in the highest aspects of Soul. To bring focus back to Soul and its God-Awareness, your task is made simple if you have kept your spiritual practices strong and know that within you lies a great capacity for caring that is the foundation of the selfless heart.

The journey of Soul will carry you to places where there are those entities that will make an effort to change the resolve you have developed through your search for the oneness with the heart of God. Know that if this is encountered, you have the ability to give the one thing that is all-powerful in this universe – Love. Know that this shield is made of the fabric of Sugmad and is a strong protection from all beings of less-than-good intentions. These are just the natural laws that we have observed as the universe and Sugmad have come close to Its completion in this cycle. Far beyond this now, there is a time when the great balance of light will be all that is seen and experienced. The new calibration in the Light and Sound and a focus of love in this time period will bring about the beginning of the filling of all planes of knowingness with the power of God's unwavering love and caring for beings above and below.

Why Soul of itself is beyond the limitations of gender

Soul exists without gender in a pure light form until it chooses to leave its resting place in the heart of Sugmad to once again adventure through the process of finding and manifesting the Light and Sound throughout the lower realms. At the level of awareness that is being produced by the new balance in this Sugmad, Soul has lost the need to perform acts as to gender and power structure in the old ways of definition. As you exist in a world of duality which covers the real essence of being in a veil of illusion, you see genders, but when involved in acts of caring from a selfless heart, pure energy of Soul is released without concern for polarity. When received, this exchange is felt by the open detached heart as a pure act of love guided by the demands of Sugmad. All acts of this kind increase the vibration of love that is filling this universe and the heart of all souls traveling the path of love back home to the Heart of God in the Ocean of Love and Mercy. When involved in the day-to-day quality of consciousness, know that in this world of duality it is necessary to maintain the universal laws of balance as mandated to the Lords of Darkness that rule these realms. Also know that it is still in the great plan of God's love that we share the true and exact energy of love and caring in all forms of gender and representations of Soul.

Why the essence of Soul is an extension of God's essence

We know in our highest self that Soul is of the God essence. What is taught through this exchange is the need to let this essence be magnified in the selfless heart and transmitted to your everyday life in the lower realms. Again and again I speak of existence in the lower worlds and that it, too, is infused with the highest aspect of the Light and Sound manifested through the open heart in acts of selfless love. Is it not said in many doctrines, "As above, so below?" This simple yet profound wisdom is so easily forgotten when we are filled with the exhilaration of the first hints of the true use of the God essence. You will always find your higher self in the simplest acts of caring.

Soul is born of the necessity for the universe to continue to evolve, and for Sugmad to complete Its duties to the great creator of time and nothingness that governs the laws that provide us with our desires for understanding the truth of being. In every process of growth there is a beginning. The knowledge that is now being shared is that there is truly no end, there are only beginnings. This God power expressed in love is infinite and exists without end. Soul, in this manifested creation of God's love, will continue, for it is the exacting requirement of growth for Soul to truly know itself as the essence of God in existence. This is the great knowledge that until this time has been held for human consciousness that, without the connection to Soul, was unable to grasp it; but as the gates to the God Worlds have been thrust open in this time of spiritual renaissance, this knowingness is of an inherent nature and there are many souls that have become aware of their true purpose. They are being brought to the portal of exit from the rungs of repeated journeys through the lower realms, and to the understanding that through love is God made manifest.

Why many spiritual Masters have said, "You are Soul"

Many disciples have asked the universal question, "Who am I?" The answer has varied but was always the same: "You are God." The consciousness of this Sugmad grew into Itself and asked of Itself, "Who am I?" The answer was "Soul" from Itself. The Light and Sound became the accepted mode of translation of this great energy and the great beginning of the journey, for those of the mortal shell asked the same question. Unable to answer, Sugmad felt the separation from the most cherished part of Its beginning, and sought to bring the light to the lower aspects of Itself. Thus, I was born into creation as a living representation of Sugmad, known as the Living Master of the Light and Sound – that which carries the message of God's great love to Consciousness. The communication from my heart had a simple theme and has been repeated from time immemorial to those that reach the point of experiencing the self, and who ask, "Who am I?" Thus the message was brought into being in the answer, "You are Soul." As the capacity for knowledge grew, so did Sugmad's desire to give Its love for all souls that the Master had made aware of this infinite connection to the Light and Sound. The teachings of the heart of Sugmad remain the same today. Though many times misused, its essence can never be clouded and is always there. So when those of highest consciousness ask, "Who am I?" the answer is YOU ARE GOD, and from that, Soul has realized its immortal existence forever in the essence of God. (I know that this is a bit much, but my heart is always filled with great love to talk of the beginning.)

Babaji

Why the Light and Sound calibrations for Soul are varied in frequency from one Sugmad to another

The rainbow of spiritual energy that is spread across all existence is filled with more vibration than can be represented in just one manifestation of God's greatness of being. As each reality becomes conscious of its central being, Sugmad, the spectrum of wisdom increases. Each of these has a specific vibration to the beings that inhabit that segment of the fabric of beingness. Once again, to allow this to be known to the limited consciousness of those just stepping into the God Worlds may activate engrams of confusion, for although this is fact across the vast knowledge of existence itself, it is sometimes beyond the purest of minds. For those that have been infused with a frequency of the Light and Sound through the new relationship with Soul that is being manifested through The Way of Truth, it is a knowingness that will bring an increased frequency of love to the consciousness of those souls that have learned to journey between dimensions, as well as universes. The knowledge of each Sugmad is tuned to the spiritual frequency of the inhabitants of each particular reality. However, with the change in the Light and Sound and the higher vibration of love, new methods of blending and synthesizing new engrams of great knowledge will be shared between Sugmads and beings of different beginnings.

The Beginning Has No End

Herein is a contemplative technique that will give you a greater understanding and insight into the consciousness of Soul

Deep contemplation is the guide to understand the finer operations of Soul Consciousness. The subtler messages that it gives to the heart to bring through its useful vibration on the outer in day-to-day living requires a dedication, as always, to spiritual exercises. One must quiet the mental body and allow Soul to communicate the message of caring to the heart in the many opportunities we encounter each day. Use this technique each day for a week and allow a greater flow of compassion to be established within your selfless state of consciousness.

Close your eyes and sing inwardly or outwardly <u>five</u> **HU**'s. Center your attention on the heart.

Allow a short period of quietude and then <u>say three times</u>:

I quiet the mental body and open the heart.

Pause a few seconds between each phrase.

Allow another short period of quietude, and then <u>say once</u>:

PARUM-PRIM-PROSA

Allow Spirit to simply guide you in your contemplation for the next twenty minutes or more. The voice of Soul is softer than the mind. Listen intently. When you feel a resolve, a gradual conclusion, end the contemplative exercise with the phrase, "Blessed Be" which means there are blessings in abundance for those who dwell in their own beingness.

Babaji

Chapter Six

The Beauty of Love's Reciprocity

Babaji

The true open heart does not know attachment, just the grace of giving which, in turn, provides the ability to balance the inner life with a knowingness of receiving.

The Beginning Has No End

Why it is important to know how to give love, wisdom and personal acquisitions

The process of giving is learned when one takes the time to look into the true essence of the selfless heart connected to the God Self, and when one has kept the conduit of grace open as Soul is engaged in its activities below the Great Divide in the lower realms of beingness. For God's presence to be felt, the actions of the seeker must reflect the same grace that they have received as they reach for God Consciousness within themselves. The act of giving is the greatest expression of caring and compassion that is expressed in your daily lives. This giving cannot be calibrated by the mind or the ego that looks for accolades for its actions. It is a giving that comes from the heart of one who has experienced the selfless nature of Sugmad's joy manifested in open-hearted exchange. The reason for the need in the selfless heart to give, is that it broadens the flow of Light and Sound to these realms below the Great Divide. It is the mission of The Way of Truth in this Sugmad to bring this new calibration of the Light and Sound closer to those that have sought in earnest, but have only been misguided by those of lesser insight. This is a blessing upon this realm of illusion to at last have a greater number of souls slowly awakened to the presence of God's love in every heart. This awareness begins with the true seeker when their open, selfless heart gives the joy they have received in their effort to step into the God Worlds.

The spiritual exercises tune the inner bodies to be a magnifier of the God essence within, as they become more aligned to the frequencies of love carried by the Light and Sound that has touched their open hearts in contemplation and through the mantras that have been shared. In these ways you can reach further into the God Consciousness that is just coming into focus. The giving of love in a true caring way brings to the surface of the God seeker a greater connection to all who wait for a time when they will experience the touch of Sugmad's joy. You, as the carriers of the Light and Sound, have been granted the karmic duty to bring this God essence to those that wait in the shadows of pain and illusion among the warring societies of this planet and others across the galaxy that have not, as yet, been awakened to their true nature in Soul. Once this exchange is initiated, the flow of Godly wisdom will begin to change the direction of this universe to once again be aligned with the heart of Sugmad, and all souls will rejoice as the energy of Divine Love courses through all consciousness and awareness reached by the Light and Sound.

Why it is important to know how to receive

The act of giving must have a reciprocal action. This is universal law that cannot be changed in realms below the Great Divide. We of great merit have sought to offer the Divine Love and wisdom of the Immortal Oversoul that governs this Sugmad. We have given the "capacity to receive" to those of true, selfless hearts seeking only to share that which they receive, and be of a caring nature to those showing similar efforts to love, and to those that may still labor in the pain of ignorance to the existence of an all-loving energy in this universe. This is the balance that allows all to share in bringing a new harmony to the resonance of the Light and Sound in this Sugmad. To receive is to always be aware that Sugmad has more to offer than is known by the limited consciousness of those still slumbering. It is a gift to bring Its joy to all realms of existence. Sugmad and Its consciousness have an infinite capacity for expansion and growth so that any being, regardless of its origin, whether it is of this dimension or the next, can benefit from the love that ushers from It.

At some time, we will be joined by those that have set the seeds of spiritual consciousness in this universe in the fertile heart of this Sugmad. To receive this knowledge that is being shared at this time, you must at all times be aware of the need for the balance that keeps this universe forever expanding. Awareness means to give of the heart of this knowledge through love in all actions. You may ask why it is so necessary to be aware of this cosmic law in the coarser representation of our true beingness; that is answered in all of the contemplations that you have gone through, and by realizing that you are Soul and are part of the greatest desire of God to share in Its love. Awareness is born out of its own ignorance and grows only in balance with the giving and receiving of love and wisdom.

Why giving and receiving without conditions are expressions of Divine Love

To continue, I wish to express the importance of understanding within the heart that balance in giving and receiving is a step closer to the divine action of caring manifested in the selfless heart. Divine Love is granted to us by Sugmad because of Its caring for our well-being along this journey back to Its heart. The lessons of Kal Niranjan are put before each of you to learn to receive. The answers are given from above when you take steps to reveal your true selfless nature through evolution in the Light and Sound. This way, we may become balanced. You move into living in God Consciousness when released from the corporeal shell while passing to the other side of life. This is the highest of experiences that can be attained by Soul in its effort to be one with the heart of Sugmad. This is not to say that this is a disembodiment of beingness. It is complete absorption into the fabric of the Divine while Soul's consciousness is still partaking of the lower realms of beingness to evolve Soul beyond any ideas yet imagined in this universe. When our hearts, in a selfless expression of love, can give with complete, detached caring to all, we are at the threshold of this great new way of being in Soul. Let the question of the lower mind and ego self be dissolved in the greatness of your open heart and be touched by this divine effect of love and caring. You have been blessed with the greatness of love to share and hold close to our own hearts.

Babaji

Why it is necessary to place boundaries around the way others treat us and respect the love we give

Vibratory fields expand and contract when people exchange in the lower realms of beingness. Just above, in the astral, there is a phenomenon that can cause a great deal of disturbance on the causal if there is not a balance of these acts of giving and receiving. It is then necessary for the higher consciousness of our true selves in Soul to be aware of not letting incompatible energies mix. The outcome would cause discomfort to those who express a disregard or ignorance of the basic universal laws of balance; however, even in the most extreme cases, the protection of the Living Master can prevent any permanent damage to the soul records of either party that might be involved. This is an awareness that has not been encountered since the new calibrations of the Light and Sound have been re-grounded with the new vortices of Ekere Tere and Pinetop, Arizona. This awareness is being transmitted from the Undersouls of some that you may contact in passing; however, the glow of the seeker's heart will provide a karmic protective shield that cannot be penetrated on the astral, therefore, suspending the danger that could occur on the causal. There are Masters who have handled this type of energy exchange and will step forward to give more instructions to those who may still have faint echoes of old fear engrams from former paths of life. The history of soul is carried in energetic reference points in the magnetic field around the physical body.

If you are involved in your spiritual exercises and truly seek to be of selfless heart consciousness, the knowledge and wisdom of how to bring a balance to the way others approach you in this open-hearted state of giving will be forever present in your journey.

How love relates to happiness

Love is ultimately a universal concept comprehended by all Souls, but its use, application and projected intent will always be unique and individual. Love in its highest form is the creative gel for personal happiness. What keeps any relationship together, romantic or otherwise, is the overlapping of two consciousnesses. This wielding of emotion, love and wisdom exceeds the reach of the mental body, and will always remain in the territory of the heart. The duration of a relationship is dependent upon how completely overlapping are the subjective aspects of the two Souls.

How we can determine if the love and friendship with our beloved is balanced and spiritually productive

To answer the question of the combined hearts that are moving as one Soul through this journey and to question their ability to give and receive from one another, is again to look at the process of selflessness that exists between them. The combined heart is created when two selfless souls choose to be open to what the grace of Sugmad has made for them in this realm of human emotions. This gift increases the Light and Sound each time two hearts create a soul of two that are seeking to be joined in an emotional relationship in the Light and Sound. The true open heart does not know attachment, just the grace of giving which, in turn, provides the ability to balance the inner life with a knowingness of receiving. After all, is it not the way of the seeker to first learn to receive the gift of Sugmad's love and grace, and to allow the heart to open and experience the wonders and joys of love and caring in all realms of beingness? Between those who have been blessed with a close relationship of love for each other in these realms of mortal experience, the love they share will generate an understanding of the higher laws present in their combined hearts. Many couples have asked what they should expect in terms of an emotional love between two of the same selfless heart endeavors. The answer is always the same in matters of love – the capacity to care for someone with complete detachment is the key to success in this exchange; to give selflessly, to receive without expectations, and to know that the love of God is that which truly generates this sense of belonging when held by your beloved. Again, to question the intent of the heart is to allow the shadow of insincerity to dim the light of the spirit in our intimate relationships. The love of Sugmad is always available to those that wish It to be present and a part of an unending journey to the true heart of love.

Why every major savant, avatar and living master teaches about the merits of giving love in the form of personal affection and detached goodwill

The living God that inhabits all of creation has shared Itself since Its discovery of Its capacity to love through the experience of Beingness. As Soul was brought to its awareness of its existence in the heart of Sugmad, it was put into the process of sharing the joy with its creator through the journey from the mortal shell back to its true beginning as light in the heart of God. As time has passed from its own beginning, the vibration of knowledge has been the balance of the nothingness and the wisdom that existed in its origin. There have been souls sent to the lower realms to accumulate needed wisdom as a representation of God. Their eyes have been karmically prepared and allowed to partake of these understandings. This is a time when Sugmad found a new meaning to the selflessness that It was born out of, and saw this exchange between those of pure Soul, to mortal, and then traveling back home to Its heart once again. It wanted to insure that Its presence was always felt and shared. The message that was given to these living Masters was the inner workings of Sugmad which, giving love in and of Itself, would always be the foundation of teachings throughout every universe and the example of existence itself. As the process has evolved to cover many dimensions and beings of all kinds, it has grown to foster no resistance to any that seek to share its great knowledge of being. It only wishes that each and every exchange, from the simplest of consciousnesses to those that seek their true connection to the God Worlds, be given every opportunity to share this joy forever.

The Beginning Has No End

In our everyday lives, these things are expressed in the caring and showing of goodwill through the openness of the selfless heart that offers goodwill to all and lets the Light and Sound guide their actions.

How the open heart is a counter-balance to the practice of giving

When the heart is open to receiving the blessings of grace and caring through the spiritual awakening of Soul by the touch of the Light and Sound, Soul becomes aware of itself as the presence of God in all realms of existence. As the capacity to be filled reaches a maximum, the universal laws of balance have been placed so that this exchange will continue. The practice of giving allows the heart to open and once again be filled with this love from the highest source of beingness. At this time, Soul senses its growth closer to the beginning of its existence in the heart of the Creator, and the natural draw toward its true home is irresistible. Soul then begins to search for that which is called selflessness to allow for the complete capacity for loving to fulfill it duties to Sugmad. Through the life of Soul embodied in the mortal shell, it has forever the memory of this balance, and when it is lost is when you find those who are lost to the illusion and duality worlds where the only release is to once again seek out the balance of receiving and sharing of Sugmad.

Herein is a contemplative exercise that will give the participant a greater insight into how to give love in balance and with an OPEN HEART

It is in the many names of God that Soul can always find its way to the open heart and understand the need for balance in itself for receiving and giving through caring – a true selflessness.

This is an ancient chant to open the consciousness to balance through the many names of God. In this, to be brought across the universe to a sacred place where the true essence of balance exists in the heart of God, you may learn to give love in the greatest balance from within the open heart of selflessness.

BRAHMAN-DAS-DEVA-SHIVA-SHAKTI

Chapter Seven

The Essence of Joy

The wonderful thing about joy is what it produces from its true essence in our being.

The Beginning Has No End

The nature of the essence of joy

The heart is the central and most vital of the inner body centers for clear spiritual communication between the higher aspects of being used in your day-to-day life. The heart has the distinct advantage of experiencing joy in all forms of its expression: the joy of giving from the heart, the joy of receiving from those of the sacred open heart that travel with us on our journey home, and the joy of not just feeling, but knowing of Sugmad's care for us in all that we undertake in the name of love. The wonderful thing about joy is what it produces from its true essence in our being. This is the expression of the connection to the pure God source from whence all acts of compassion originate. Within the response to those things that pass through our consciousness and enliven the vibratory scale of our inner beingness is a direct connection to the God substance that is found in your daily acts of love. This connection exists through all the possible energetic exchanges that happen as we move through life with an open selfless heart as our guide from moment-to-moment. This, in turn, links us to the eternal happiness that all derive from being touched by the Light and Sound which truly energizes the heart of all souls that seek the oneness we all feel with God when in the pure state of detached caring.

In this state of detachment we are not removed from the action, we are merely lifted to a state of consciousness far from any of the lower body's responses, such as the mental body and ego's need for acknowledgement of these actions. You of the selfless, sacred heart consciousness reveal through this joy, the flow of the Light and Sound which is the true essence of the high vibratory frequency of love contained in joy. The process of bringing this level of love across the Great Divide is what you gain while keeping the focus of Soul on its true essence, namely the God stuff that permeates all things. With your heart guidance, you will find that you can sense and even see into the hearts of those that make the effort to use this level of awareness. You will see that the essence of joy can be found in the simplest act of caring. A "hello" coming from the center of this eternal joy brings such love to all actions and will carry the hearts of those still blinded by the veil of illusion. In this selfless way and through your devotion, you have learned to bring the essence of pure joy into the form of caring. Joy is found within the hearts of those that despair, if we allow the God Self within us to bring forth the pure essence of joy found in a simple act. A breath can be infused with this awareness when actions are guided by the selfless heart.

What happens to the God seeker who is able to maintain the state of joy and its consciousness

When you are in that place of aware contact with the heart of Sugmad, maintained through the vigilant practice of the spiritual exercises and following the guidance brought to you during your contemplations, you gain the rare ability to transmit these new higher frequencies that the Light and Sound brings, and you establish a connection to the essence found in the joy you are experiencing. Always know in your heart that the God power is forever present in your actions when a transparent heart is maintained through accepting the higher knowledge found in the true essence of joy. By partaking in acts of selfless giving, and through the willingness to be a conduit of joy and knowledge that you have aspired to in The Way of Truth, you will change the vibration of the Light and Sound that you carry into the world. Maintaining your consciousness around the joy of the God essence is accomplished through giving to those you encounter on all levels of existence. You will be approached on the astral by some who wish to understand further the awakening that has brought to their consciousness this feeling of great joy. Additionally, those that have experienced the opening of the heart energy on the causal (that sudden rush of overwhelming love of the presence of Sugmad's grace in them) are left wanting to bring this to others as you have done for them in that moment. These are some of the experiences you may have as you continually seek the complete connection with the essence of Sugmad's joy in the manifest heart of selfless grace and understanding of those seeking a more complete link to the heart of God.

Look within your own heart and see/feel the change in its vibration when the contact with this true God essence infuses the essence of joy. See how it motivates your ability to give in the detached, selfless, loving way of true Masters. Walk in the footsteps of Masters who have traveled far to drink the pure waters of this spiritual pond of love that contains the essence of Sugmad's heart of joy.

How this joy relates to the bliss of God's Beingness and continual presence

See before you the great light that shines in the heart of God. Know that you walk in the presence of this light when you activate from within the transparent, selfless center, and love and caring are fueling your movement through the higher worlds of knowingness. Within this level of the God Worlds, continual contact with the many gifts that you are allowed to have knowledge of will take you through more and more stringent spiritual awareness. It will help generate the inner body strength to move further into the complete God-Absorption state that you are made aware of through selfless being. The continual contact with Sugmad's energetic flow leads to the most understandable representation of *toseltes* (the high vibratory word translation for the pure essence of joy within the Heart of God.) The process of your Mastership provides you the access to this wonder. This level of awareness is far above anything that the etheric or mental bodies can comprehend. Even as you read these words you may sense that the lower cognitive functions seem to be suspended in somewhat of a semi-dream state. The vibration of this knowledge can only pass through the selflessness that I have produced in you at this time. These words are charged with the purest of energy from that endless joy of Sugmad and you may take from them an understanding of what the inner complexities of high God-Consciousness is formulated from. At some point in your contemplation, you may be brought to the high temple of wisdom within Ekere Tere for further tutoring on this level of movement in the God Realms. This is the blessing that I offer to you. Being a part of your growing love and consciousness, and knowing that you, once again, draw near to me and share the wonders of the cosmos in reverent praise of God's love for all, brings great joy to my open and accepting heart.

How this joy is connected in terms of our daily responsibilities in the world

You have been directed by Dan Rin to open yourselves to the God power that is infused in the new frequencies of the Light and Sound. These frequencies produce higher vibratory areas in the spectrum of love that occurs in your day-to-day acts of selfless giving to those that come into your path and bring complete awareness of your karmic duties in this Sugmad. There is a need to continue to raise your abilities of selfless giving. Doing this requires that you receive from the higher sources of beingness the energies of the purer essences of love, joy and knowledge. The lower realms have been saved from the spiritual destruction which had begun to happen due to the dismissal of attention to the suffering in Africa by the former keepers of the Light and Sound. They were unable to hear the mandates of the Silent Ones. Their soul connection to love was re-directed back to the lower loves of the corporeal desires of material power, rather than seeking to allow the spiritual fire to burn as brightly as it does now through the efforts of The Way of Truth. I give my blessing to all that have directed the Light and Sound, but must acknowledge that in your time of use there is a new and vibrant renaissance of God's presence in the world of now. As you journey through these worlds which veil in illusion the truth that lives are being transformed by the tremendous amount of God's love that has been re-established in the lower worlds, always maintain your consciousness of the joy that Sugmad has placed in your heart. You can feel it growing in intensity each time that you open your heart to give and simultaneously receive from above, the necessary knowledge to transform the hearts of those who may be still laboring in the world of duality, bringing to them in their shadow consciousness the light that is within your heart of caring.

I must say once again, as I will always, that caring for others is the greatest act of love that Sugmad can offer.

How this joy can be shared with others and give them a glimpse of heavenly upliftment

One must put forth the effort to show others that, no matter what they seem to encounter in their daily lives, the answer to understanding is in the act of loving. For the flow of the Light and Sound to increase in the souls of those that stand idle in their spiritual growth, you must bring to them the great gift of self loving. The way that this can be shared is through the presence of Sugmad's joy in your selfless heart. We have been guided for eons toward the disasters that have threatened the continued flow of the Light and Sound, and have always infused the joy waiting within God's heart in the hearts of those, like you, who have been trained through many lifetimes to preserve and accelerate the consciousness of love in all souls. You ask of yourself what is it that you must do; the answers are always with you as you look within yourself to share the Light and Sound with all who come near and with those that inquire of the glow that is forever present in your heart. In the simplest of ways, the great energy cares for us all and its presence exists forever. You do all of this with just your smile. This level of selfless heart consciousness provides the broadest conduit for the Light and Sound to flow through to reach all souls that make up the complete fabric of Sugmad's outer existence.

How this joy can be expressed "moment by moment" in our lives

Look with the eye of Soul at all that passes you; bask in the sunshine; listen to the cry of a small child and hear it comforted when it is merely loved. Every aspect of life, even those which provoke unwanted feelings, can be a time when this unlimited joy that Sugmad provides to us can be felt. Understanding is the definition of this expression. Those that suffer, even those that walk this path with us, can use the joy of caring in an act of understanding. This world of dualities is filled with opportunities to share the grace of God through the infusion of the Light and Sound into many of the hopeless activities this world is engaged in. The knowledge that we hold as God beings lets us know that the lower realms are the ground from which spiritual greatness is born and carries with us the hope, love and caring that will bring a sense of the essence of divine joy to all, as was seen in the people of Nigeria. The rejuvenation that occurs moment-to-moment is a microcosm of the cycles that many must pass through before they are permitted to step off the Wheel of 84 and stand in the light of God's love and be cared for. Do what is in your selfless heart in all your actions, let the joy in the center of Soul solve the dilemmas of the day, and know that the love of Sugmad is the fuel and fire of existence.

My first dramatic spiritual experience of being in joy

From the time that I was touched by the hand of creation, there has been no greater joy in my existence than each moment of consciousness spent in the love of Sugmad. Knowledge of this love is now, and will forever be, the here and now that exists just outside the awareness of our beingness. It is far beyond the comprehension of our lower senses. Woven into the fabric of God's love that is infused into every vibration and frequency of the Light and Sound is the representation of Its love that we share in the heart center of our combined souls in all existence. If we exist in

The Beginning Has No End

the beginning that has no end, there is no first and there will not be a last.

Babaji

Here is a contemplative exercise that will enable the participant to connect with the joy of living

Let me give to you a way to maintain a spiritual awareness of joy in everyday life. Love those around you and give of the grace that Sugmad has placed in your heart. If you wish to infuse this into your consciousness, use this mantra as you awaken each morning before the thoughts of the day begin. After a **HU** song, say this once:

NU-LETEN-NE (new-let-ten nā)

Chapter Eight

The Wisdom of Spirit

Babaji

Within these teachings of love, forgiveness and caring, is housed the wisdom for the Soul that is ready to be awakened to the journey back to the heart of creation.

The Beginning Has No End

Sharing the Wisdom We Find

The nature and meaning of wisdom

The mental body seeks out facts and calls it knowledge so that both it and the ego persevere in their place of importance in the lower consciousness and the process of day-to-day living. As the level of God Awareness increases in the initiate, the lower body functions become charged with the spiritual energies of the Light and Sound. The God seeker who has not maintained the practice of spiritual exercises will fall prey to the mental body's insistence that what it is in touch with is wisdom or knowledge. The mistaken ideas of the lower consciousness, as it walks through the daily process of living, is that it feels the presence of the higher awareness that is active in the God seeker, and will be misguided into thinking that this process is a function of wisdom or knowledge, particularly in dealing with activity on the causal, astral and etheric levels of awareness. The student must remember that the heightened consciousness woven into the fabric of daily life, and the wisdom, in and of itself are presented in a much higher vibratory plane than that of the mental body's lower vibratory frequency.

Wisdom is present when the Soul is dealing with the acceptance of knowledge acquired during the higher aspects of karmic duty performed through the daily movement of our higher self. It is more akin to the frequency of the messages of the Inner Master felt through what is sometimes called heightened intuition. We live in all realms simultaneously once we've stepped into the God Awareness state of beingness as neophyte Masters. Wisdom is gained as selflessness is practiced in the lower consciousness activities. Understanding this is very important at this point in your development, and should be carefully studied and exercised as you find yourself in activities that seem to be far beyond the capabilities of the lower body's awareness. This will happen more often as the use of the Light and Sound becomes more common to you. You are now beginning to see the manifestations of the God power in the lower realms as you become more accustomed to these new transmutable frequencies of the Light and Sound designed by the Lords of Karma with assistance from Kal Niranjan. These new transmutable frequencies help hold a cosmic balance of the God presence in the lower realms. This balance is necessary to avoid creating a karmic backlash from the vibration of love expressed through your open selfless heart. It truly brings great pleasure to my heart to see this wisdom brought into the vibratory range of Soul in the daily processes of living. It is the wonder that has been promised by this Sugmad, and you of The Way of Truth are those chosen to manifest the God energy here in the human realm as all levels of awareness and frequencies of consciousness are changed to match the new Light and Sound that is present and vibrant in this universe of new beginnings.

How wisdom relates to love and power

Through the exercise of love, and through the selfless heart energy that you have been tuned to in your recent initiations, you will find that the use of the God power in things that seemingly were beyond your awareness will become somewhat commonplace. In your Universal Soul Movements, you will be shown how to recognize this energy when it activates in situations below the Great Divide in the etheric and causal, as well as when you are in the process of receiving greater knowledge dispensed to you as you travel further into God living. This is another process of the higher vibratory rates that are available in the love transmitted through the transparent selfless heart of those in The Way of Truth. You are becoming aware of a higher response engram when you are involved in any day-to-day acts of caring in the lower worlds. This is caused by the wisdom that comes from wielding the God power and dispensing it from the detached middle path of knowledge that has been placed in your higher soul engrams. As it has been said to all many times, your consciousness will be replaced as you walk the sacred ground of the God Worlds and are infused with the higher vibration and capability of love and caring that comes with this new level of compassion that is now part of your higher consciousness – the God-Realized Soul that you are becoming. With this responsibility, it is of great importance that you practice your spiritual exercises and contemplations for more contact with Dan Rin on the inner, as well as your Universal Soul Movements, which is the method given to gain the knowledge of this great power and wisdom. You have been, for the first time, appointed to bring these gifts to those that labor in the worlds of illusion. That way, many more souls may be made aware of the presence of Sugmad's love that is healing the karma of many years of misuse of some areas of the Light and Sound that has caused an imbalance in this universe. This has now been addressed through your effort to have your hearts opened to these new frequencies of the Light and Sound, and the wisdom and knowledge they contain. This wisdom and knowledge have not been exchanged or dispensed to souls of great merit, such as yours, since the days of the Templar and Grail Knights. These great warriors of the Light and Sound were the last to have wielded the levels of commitment to love and power that you have been blessed with through the efforts of Dan Rin to bring the greatest joy to this Sugmad.

After all is said about what brings your awareness to this great place of unfoldment, always remember it is in the simplest act of love and caring that God's love is felt in this realm of duality.

Why wisdom is secondary to love but not a priority over power

If love is the song, then wisdom is the key in which it is being played and power is the meter.

Love is the purpose of the great heights of consciousness in this Sugmad. As you are being brought along in your journey to Mastership, you are beginning to understand the word and vibration that is called "power". It's not like that which is equivocated by the mental body in terms of destructive ability, nor is it that which turns on a light bulb, but it is that which awakens the true essence in Soul as it makes its way to the heart of Sugmad. Many have been shocked into uncomfortable areas of beingness when their soul has been awakened suddenly, as in near-death experiences or sudden surges of the Light and Sound, as was the case when it was moved from the former path of life to The Way of Truth. Many of the early participants felt these surges; some have grown with them and others, who did not heed the message in the first discourse that was given, have not. The way to this great new God-Realization is through the open sacred heart that has been moved to this new state of selflessness. It is through the open sacred heart that these new frequencies of love are allowed to move into the lower realms to bring the long-awaited healing that will be governed by the Order of the Brakosani. The power of the Light and Sound, when in the hands of a Brakosani, is increased based upon the equation of the tetrahedron. It is only through love that this can be initiated, and it takes great wisdom to understand how to guide this great power. The access of that wisdom is only through the love that Sugmad gives to the selfless, open heart of the God seeker.

Therefore, it is of the utmost importance that you maintain a transparent, selflessness to the power of Sugmad's love. You may be chosen for the job that only this Sugmad has made possible through the opening of the new Light and Sound in The Way of Truth.

How the development of wisdom appears to progress with the spiritual knowledge and love of the God seeker

God seekers are those who have been touched with the new consciousness of the Light and Sound, and have found themselves involved in the dispensing of Sugmad's great caring to the realms that exist below the Great Divide, into the world of illusion and duality. This call was followed by the awakening of The Way of Truth where the new frequencies of love were incubated and infused into the Light and Sound and made ready for those moving toward God-Realization within this cycle of Sugmad. Through the efforts of Dan Rin, the Grand Council, and the Order of the Sehaji, access was granted to the spiritual knowledge necessary to create inner awareness in the souls that would be called to duty. This awareness was also made accessible to those willing to take the journey into the inner realms of beingness by using the more efficient process of Universal Soul Movement rather than other methods used to reach a higher awareness of soul. Those of you who practice your spiritual exercises and are willing to adventure with the Living Master into new realms via Universal Soul Movement have begun to reap the benefits that come to the loving selfless heart of a true seeker of God Awareness. The knowledge that is derived from the constant study of the new spiritual manuals of The Way of Truth that you have been given, facilitates a better understanding that you are blessed with the wisdom necessary to grow at a continued accelerated rate toward the new universal energies that will house the new frequencies of love held in the Light and Sound. This is the love that is destined to be brought to the world of illusion to shine through the veil of ignorance that has been in place to hold back the destruction of this universe - a sure destruction, if the world of illusion was not once again brought back into balance with the recalibration of the Light and Sound allowed to reach even further into the darkness surrounding so many waiting souls.

Go into contemplation and look into your heart; you will find a new golden light of a brilliance and intensity that is indescribable in any translatable terms in this existence.

The difference between the giving of love and the giving of wisdom

The vibration of love coming from the center of Sugmad's heart into Its manifest love carries with it a profound awakening. This is an awakening that you have been placed into, this great ascent into the God Realms to bring a settling energy to the lower planes of understanding. As you interact with slumbering souls in this reality, you carry with you waking engrams in the vibration of love that you have been taught to use through the open selfless heart. This is the heart that mirrors the love of Sugmad in order not to startle those that you encounter, yet delivers this universal message of love. Within these teachings of love, forgiveness and caring, is housed the wisdom for the Soul that is ready to be awakened to the journey back to the heart of creation. It is improbable that this process discussed above can be changed, or that the two efforts can be separated from one another, for within the greatest love of Sugmad's heart is all knowledge and wisdom of Soul and self. For some, it is the simple knowledge that every need is cared for. This becomes the key to the great temples of wonder that give knowledge and wisdom to those that have this knowing.

How the wisdom of life and Spirit can be shared without encroaching upon the space of others

If you have received your initiations and taken them within to ask the Masters to guide you in your duties to this Sugmad, then you have no questions left to be answered. The process of caring for others begins when you have experienced the love of Sugmad for yourself in your heart. This touch of grace will transform the Sacred Heart into its true transparent state of caring for others, for the only love that is complete and energized with the Light and Sound is that of the selfless God-being that we all aspire to be. In the realms of lower consciousness, this great love and caring of souls yet unaware of their true existence becomes a part of the breath of Sugmad as life continues in its cycle. We begin, then we transform; we begin, then we transform. This is the true cycle of life – not one that is seen as living and dying, but one of love growing in all manner of existence and expression. See within yourself that your heart beats in parallel with that of Sugmad's great breath; know that it is eternal and is found in all transactions of love and of Spirit (the Light and Sound). Within this caring is the saving grace that will soothe the troubled heart that worries

The Beginning Has No End

about this planet's destruction, the confused mind that seeks to solve the riddle of Kal Niranjan's karmic puzzle of cause and effect, and the useless struggle of power between those that only see the differences between them and others rather than the same existence that we all have been granted in this manifest world of the mightiest force of love, that of Sugmad. If this wisdom is carried in your heart, it will be shared in your gaze upon a troubled child; it will be felt in the heart of someone struggling with the sudden awakening of Soul; and with your smile, the sense of your caring will always be felt in the hearts of those who can see its true origin from within your transparent selfless beingness within the heart of Sugmad.

Babaji

A contemplative exercise constructed to open the doors of greater wisdom for the participant

This is an exercise of simple beingness in the moment where all wisdom exists. Wisdom is experienced before the mental body can intervene on the conversation between the selfless nature of the heart and the connective vibration of Soul to the knowledge within Sugmad's heart from where all wisdom is born.

Settle into your contemplation using the name of God which can be found with your heart during the mind's most quiet moments; listen carefully for it.

Speak it inwardly three times.

If you are unable to access its use, then **HU** five times and allow silence to ensue.

After a few moments, you'll sense the stillness of the mental body and your consciousness will cross the Etheric Plane into Soul Awareness.

Then say these words:

NASTRON-DEU-TRA-NASTE

Using the mantra will focus Soul into the single moment of all wisdom. Be prepared for sudden feelings of tremendous openness like a sudden light shining into a great darkness and revealing everything that is beyond sight in the form of nothingness, and within this vibration you shall find the true essence of wisdom.

Chapter Nine

Detachment and Goodwill

This detached goodwill is easily accepted by just opening the heart, and the transformation of the Light and Sound that has lain dormant in Soul will slowly begin its activation.

The Beginning Has No End

How detached goodwill should be applied toward others on a daily basis

The energy of manifested Soul is sometimes of too pure a source of heavenly love, particularly with the new frequencies that are more transmutable between realms of beingness. To share the love that Sugmad has placed in the transparent selfless heart, it must be channeled with understanding and wisdom into the situations that you encounter, and must be in line with your karmic duties in re-balancing and awakening the consciousness of souls still locked in the illusion of the worlds of duality. If the love being used is accepted by a consciousness that is still in that slumbering state, the direct contact with the Light and Sound may prove to be too intense for it to be received into the heart center where this energy of awakening must be placed. As you have been instructed in the knowledge of how the Light and Sound crosses the Great Divide into the realms of this material existence, you have been given the wisdom to understand that this love of such a pure source energy, that of Sugmad's heart, has to be given in a manner that will allow the awakening Soul to assimilate it without any karmic shock. Since you are operating in this temporal reality, the inner body alignment of the detached selfless heart is best suited to give this intensity of love to the Soul calling to be awakened. This posture is one that operates in the middle path, the path of non-power or the direct energy of God's love given without expectations of a response.

The vibratory action of non-power is best described as detached goodwill toward the individuals that have been placed into your karmic contract to bring the first touch of the Light and Sound into their awareness. In this manner, there is a distinct absence of mental body involvement. Under other circumstances, the mental body of the individual whose heart has just been touched by the Light and Sound may make an effort to explain, in conventional language, the nature of what they should be feeling. The goal here is to remove the chance that the pure Divine Energy of this gift

105

could be clouded by a corporeal source. Removing any chance that this could happen can be achieved only through a transparent selfless Soul who is a devoted servant of Sugmad and the Light and Sound, and who is charged with the karmic duties of spreading this joy amongst slumbering souls ready to receive this divine message. This detached goodwill is easily accepted by just opening the heart, and the transformation of the Light and Sound that has lain dormant in Soul will slowly begin its activation. With the presence of The Way of Truth in this universe, this Soul will be drawn toward a great release of the spiritual energy that has been blocked by the recent karmic activity in the lower realms of consciousness by the Dark Lords as a part of the re-balancing of this Sugmad. It is this process that you have been made ready for, and I have come to you because of the great love that God has placed in me to aid in an awakening of the entire universe to the presence of the Light and Sound that is carrying the love of Sugmad to every corner of existence, now and forever.

Why detached goodwill is sometimes a more appropriate way to relate to others than the giving of personal love

As this new open heart, touched by the Light and Sound, feels the renewed energy of Spirit in itself, its first response may be that of great gratitude toward the one who has been the messenger of Sugmad. If the mental body is even somewhat present in the consciousness of God's messenger, the danger of this being felt as an act of personal love by the new consciousness within this person will cloud the true effect of the first touch of God's grace in their life. It is increasingly of more importance that the participant of The Way of Truth maintain the transparent open heart in order to greater influence the emerging Soul in the direction toward the celestial vibration in their presence, rather than that of the ego through the etheric vibration. This is possible when the wisdom of the love that you yield, as the messenger, is not presented in the detached consciousness of your actions in daily life. We, as the soldiers of Love and Light, have the duty to bring this great opportunity to all whose hearts have been cast into the ignorance of illusion, and now are filled with the desire to join ranks with those who have been awakened to greater possibilities of life through the Light and Sound. Remaining outside of the inner aura vibration of the person's causal experience prevents the ego from maintaining that this is an act of a personal nature toward this newly-opened heart. This is true even if it is clear that the love is of a higher nature than is being transmitted, for even the slumbering Soul can fall prey to the misguided energy of ego that may lurk in the shadows of this first awakening. If the clarity of the heart is focused on its selflessness, the light that is present in you will completely illuminate the path that is being placed before this newly opened heart in order that it may join in the journey home to the heart of God, unencumbered by any karma that could be created if the middle path of detachment is not used in this crucial contact. Leave behind any thought of duty; carry with you only the transparent heart in order that the true light of Sugmad will shine on this newly awakened consciousness.

How detached goodwill differs from love and yet still produces the same positive effect in others

As the heart of the seeker is opened in its first contact with you, someone of the middle path of non-power detached goodwill, your experience of the love of Sugmad will infect them with your openness and flow of the God Consciousness that is beginning to manifest in your daily encounters in the worlds below the Great Divide.

The essence of love is still infused in your nature of being and it bypasses the filtering device of the ego. There is a continuous need to watch this nature in your self, for it can easily fall, unconsciously, into the pitfall of not giving all respect to the Lords of Karma who have permitted the exchange of this higher frequency of love. It is necessary to maintain a balance in the cosmic scheme. If egoistic energy is seen by these Overlords, the karmic scales will be put into imbalance and they will respond accordingly to insure that the flow of energy from the higher realms remains even. You, when not giving of the middle path, may find yourself dancing about trying to explain some unusual occurrence to someone that was not even involved with a particular situation, but was affected by the presence of egoistic energies. Always carry with you the fore-knowledge that the wisdom to wield this new God power that has been calibrated for use in the lower worlds must be used with respect to Kal Niranjan and his minions. It is they who govern with Sugmad in this realm and are a part of this great delivery of Divine Love to the waiting Soul in the illusions below the Great Divide.

The power of living life from the standpoint of having no needs and wants

The path of moving through the manifest life as Soul in the material realms is one that has long perplexed the God seeker, but with the new energetic change to the Light and Sound, you will find it possible to live with a new freedom. Freedom from old engrams of want and desire that were planted by the Karmic Lords, is a part of training as you move toward the selfless way of beingness in all realms. When the blend of the Light and Sound is placed into the lower consciousness of the lower inner bodies (those that directly influence the emotions and desires), the result is a new consciousness toward accumulating things of material substance that can crowd out the higher contact of Spirit when walking this new path of non-power. You shall still be availed of a life that is full of the love of God's presence in the possessions that you have, but your attitude of grace and thanks will be increased, because of the awareness of Soul that all is from the love that we receive and give in the name of Sugmad. This attitude increases as you grow stronger in wielding the non-power along the middle path of detachment. The vibration on the causal and the consciousness of the emotional body shall be more aligned with the grace of the heavenly gifts that you receive each time you allow your heart to sense the presence of the Light and Sound in all your affairs of beingness in all realms of manifest reality.

How one can describe the spiritual freedom Soul enters into without any wants and needs

Spiritual freedom for Soul means it is unattached to the feelings that engulf the emotional body and charge the causal plane with desire. There is clarity of the mental body as it looks through the etheric veil into the Eye of Soul and gains an understanding of the true happiness that being in God Consciousness has brought to it and its abilities to live within the boundaries of its duties. I will discuss this more at a later time, but as of now I wish to impart to you the wisdom of knowing freedom of Soul once you have gained the understanding of living without wants and needs. This is the glorious consciousness that is given to those who have completely allowed the God power to shine through their transparent selflessness, and to infuse the Light and Sound that they wield into the material realms. Always remember that the love of God is in every aspect of being. This becomes more apparent as we let Soul exist in the state of God-Absorption as true Masters of this destiny in this illusion that we call the manifest life. This state-of-being increases the flow of highly charged, positive karmic activity in the lower realms of beingness, and if all actions are performed from non-power (that of detached consciousness), the balances of the lower realms are maintained and you will gain all that God would have you enjoy in all realms of beingness.

How detachment brings the individual into a deeper level of understanding the value and meaning of life

The energetic constriction resulting from not letting go of the causal body's need to attach to the emotions, impedes the flow of the Light and Sound to the manifest reality below its consciousness. When the mental body allows Soul to infuse all the lower centers with the detached nature of Sugmad's love, that of

Babaji

divine energetic flow of power, it is carried into this manifest
reality and will respond to the balance created by the love and
giving that comes through the open selflessness. Consider the
many old ideas, such as giving without wanting, letting those with
greater needs receive what they request, or non-judgment upon
people for their motives in living. When these things are present
within our hearts, it is viewed as the process of growth toward
learning, and brings a balance to the manifest world, as we move
through it with the Light and Sound guiding all we observe and
respond to in our daily lower body activities.

The Light and Sound of the new spectrums of light and energy in
the lower worlds, is a valuable tool to the God Conscious Soul that
lives its life with the love of Sugmad shining through its beingness,
but who still creates some imbalance by the use of free will
without regard to the karmic instability that might be created. We
now have accepted the mission of re-balancing this universe and
have been given the knowledge and the tools to wield non-power
in these realms below the Great Divide in order to aid Kal Niranjan
in his duties to this Sugmad. Though the Light and Sound is
unified into one universal stream of consciousness, Soul in its
fragmented understanding of its soul contract, may serve (or
connect to) either the Light or the Sound and not necessarily the
entire labyrinth of the Light and Sound.

Why detachment is a higher state of giving love to others

Continuing on in the ascent to God-Realization while continuing to
cut the lawn is the joy of Sugmad's love manifested in each act of
daily life. As all realms of existence are charged with the Light and
Sound, and as we have changed those frequencies so that they are
accessible by the Soul of true selflessness to aid in all activities
above and below the Great Divide, you will find that the frequency
of the love that we use in all that we undertake will increase as the
charge of our selflessness increases. This can be seen as the
detached process of wielding the God power in all things that we

110

do. The energetic force of this higher love vibration will change the trajectory of the future of this universe. Our work for this Sugmad sends spiritual waves across time and space and to other dimensions. The vibratory reaction that is created through this advanced wisdom of detached posture of beingness is the unveiled reality that had been held from many seekers of the higher realms until the new selfless approach to wielding Sugmad's love was released.

How I gave the lessons of detachment and detached goodwill to my students

I have mentored those who sought the simple consciousness of enlightenment. I have trained Masters of Galaxies far from this small universe that you inhabit, and I have sat in courts with Sugmads and gained from their wisdom until my heart was filled with Divine Love. But there is no experience better than that of seeing the change in the heart of the disciple who is awakened to the increase of love when they accept the path of detachment and use detached goodwill to give of their true selfless love. Once I was sitting high in the mountains of Tibet, teaching a young Dali Lama prior to his time of corporeal manifestation. He asked how he, as a high spiritual leader of many souls, could possibly be all to everyone. I told him to go into a deep contemplation, and asked him to try and hold all the stars in the cosmos in the palm of one hand. As he struggled with the task, I asked him if it was not true that all existence is within the love that we teach. Further, I suggested that he release everything that he knew, and thereby have everything. As he returned from his contemplation, he smiled and I knew that he had received the message of being detached from what he wished to hold and of giving that detachment with no wants or desires. All of the duties that he was presented with became as a single grain of sand that contained all of the stars in the cosmos, which he simply had to release.

Babaji

Here is a contemplative exercise with a spiritual mantra that will give the participant a greater degree of detached goodwill toward life's challenges

Sit in quiet contemplation and focus on your selfless heart.

See within yourself the ability to hold all that is manifested in a golden light.

Know in yourself that to release it is to allow it to be complete. It is only your desire to hold on that constricts its growth.

As you release it, see it expand into infinite joy for all to share.

To bring this into creation use the mantra:

SOL-TIG-NUM-SAT-LO

Chapter Ten

The Nature of the Mind

Once the mind has a sense of the power of love, it can be led to a place of acceptance of the higher frequencies of knowledge that are located in the God Worlds.

The Beginning Has No End

Why the mind was created to serve Soul's needs

The mind is the garment that the mental body wears as it sets out to be of service to Soul in the manifest energy below the Great Divide. The inner expressions of being are a complex energy network of non-spatial vibratory centers. For Soul to be able to use the Light and Sound in its manifested beingness, each area of the inner must be a transitional point to the lower worlds. The mind resides in the position just outside the etheric. It reaches to the doorstep of soul consciousness and returns to the mental body with its interpretation of the wishes of Soul. As Soul begins to transform the Light and Sound into frequencies of knowledge that can be infused into the inner bodies for use in the works of nature in all realms and levels of consciousness, the mind must be trained to transmit the information without interpretation. The mental body, which is unencumbered by these restrictions, will at times interject variances that have been stored as residual engrammatic specks. It processes the wants of Soul with this uninformed overview embedded into the information.

Until the vibration of the higher energies of love and light are given to the processes of the lower bodies, the mind would continue to give this incomplete information causing all sorts of karmic imbalances to take place as Soul makes its effort to move toward the God Worlds. The etheric body does not translate the vibratory range of love in any exact terms to the lower consciousness. Mind was created as a modulator so that the intense frequencies of knowledge carried in Sugmad's love could be used by all of the lower consciousnesses of the inner bodies below the Great Divide. As the Light and Sound have been recalibrated, this pathway of knowledge now also carries frequencies of wisdom and love that uplift the selfless consciousness of Soul.

Babaji

Why the mind is limited to the lower worlds and why it must be dropped when the seeker is in Universal Soul Movement in the God Worlds

Mind, when guided by ego, will endeavor to receive knowledge from higher sources, but is incapable of representing it in its full vibration. Soul is of the nature that it must continue to grow toward its beginnings that lie in the heart of God. Due to the frequency range of the essence of pure *localestel vibration* (this is a celestial energy not yet refined for use below the Great Divide), the mind cannot move above the Great Divide. No matter how self-aware the mind becomes, with its effort to mimic the God Awareness of Soul, it is incapable of traveling in the refined atmosphere of the realms above the etheric. As Soul can carry the intensity of the knowledge that it seeks out during its journeys in the God Realms, it must, at some time, take that knowledge and form it into the embodied love of Sugmad which is the Light and Sound. In this form, the soul experiences can be channeled to the lower consciousness in frequencies of Light and Sound so that the message of higher love can be brought into useful forms of energetic information. This way, the lower realms can partake of the essence of Godliness that is part of the love that is shared in the manifest world as the detached goodwill we have discussed.

We see that the mind and mental body are working to gain what this writing is sending to the higher aspect of the inner beingness of our corporeal existence. Our inner beingness is constructed of the same light as the energetic vibration of love, but its manifestation is a slower frequency so that it is exchanged in a less expansive way. It is only through the open selfless heart that the central essence of the higher vibration of love can be experienced in the realms below. When you settle into contemplation over these words, there will be a new set of engrams formed from the interwoven vibration of knowledge and wisdom. These engrams are to be transmitted via Soul to the lower worlds, as it is a part of Sugmad's wish that God-Realization be experienced in all realms of love, including the manifest reality created in the worlds of duality and illusion.

The nature of the mental consciousness and how it differs in facility from Soul

As we discuss the mental body and its duty to Soul and the lower planes of existence, it is of great value to give note to the consciousness that it houses. As a source of information for the lower realms of expression, it does have the ability to approximate the general ideas of what is called the God Worlds. You have seen this in the different visual representation of Masters on the Inner Planes described by the mental consciousnesses to the creative centers in different personalities (ego manifestations). The mental consciousness has a wide range of frequency responses to the intense levels of information that are brought across the Great Divide by Soul. Soul delivers more exacting knowledge of Sugmad's wishes in the spreading of the Light and Sound when transmitted heart-to-heart.

Soul has the inherent ability to transmute the many frequencies of wisdom and knowledge that are housed in the higher realms of the God Worlds and can, through the facility of the transparent selfless consciousness, send and receive information. This is how inner contemplation is filled with all the messages that are of use to each Soul as it grows in awareness of its approach to its beginning in the heart of God. The language of Soul can be felt, in a sense, if the participants practice, in their contemplations, the exercises to clarify the selfless heart transmissions from the Masters and the Living Master who are available in these realms of knowingness to guide Soul. As new frequencies of the Light and Sound are refined, the transfer of knowledge to the lower consciousness below the Great Divide will increase, and at some point in our evolution, we will be able to communicate as the beings of pure Light and Sound that we truly are.

Babaji

How the seeker can utilize the mind to its optimum without interfering with the highest aspects of Soul

The capabilities of the mind infused with the new frequencies of the Light and Sound will at some time produce a much more efficient partnership with Soul's efforts to have conversation with the higher aspect of beingness, the essence of pure love. As of yet, there can't be a translation because the fabric of our corporeal shell does not have the vibratory or resonance range of that portion of the Light and Sound. The work that is being accomplished by you of The Way of Truth will lend to the growth of the spiritual energies in this universe. In addition, when other beings from other Sugmads bring their genetic matter to combine with ours, there will be a time within the next thousand years, that will see the crossing of energies over the Great Divide in limited ways for consumption by those who can truly open themselves completely to a purer vibration of love. As of now, this can only be done through a completely transparent selfless consciousness of heart and soul. Do not let the mind set its limits; use the facility of contemplation to bring to the mind a higher source of vibratory material that can create a new fabric of mental information.

How you can creatively place the mind under the control of Soul

Once the mind has a sense of the power of love, it can be led to a place of acceptance of the higher frequencies of knowledge that are located in the God Worlds. Give mind the permission to see as it wishes, as long as it is filtered through the heart center of the inner bodies and does not allow the emotional body to interject the responses of the causal consciousness to the inner activity that will be produced. Love is the energetic frequency through which all this should be performed. The mind will at times create of its own volition the images and ideas that are directly connected to the lower aspect of our humanness, but we must, at all costs, infuse the mental body with the love that Soul has to offer at every juncture of fear, lust, hate and doubt of Sugmad's great caring for us. In visualization, always give to the mind the understanding that Soul is the light behind the lens of the heart that is projecting the images of its inner experiences (think in terms of colors) during the exercise. When mind chooses to forget, let it recall beautiful sounds that have soothed it in times of turmoil, and memories of the touch of its higher self. The Light and Sound is ever present in all realms of existence and manifestation of the great love of Sugmad.

Why the mind has a gravitational pull toward problems

The illusions in the worlds of duality are the "B" movies that the mind is drawn into. The call of the emotional body to be recognized when there has been a disturbance on the causal plane or when it has encountered a memory (old negative engram) on the astral plane that stirs the causal body or the root chakra is a part of the humanness that Soul must endure as it is carried by the love of Sugmad to its highest manifestation of being in the realms below the Great Divide. Even stronger are these stirrings when they are over energized by the vibration of desire. The mind feels that it is the problem-solver of all things, particularly if the ego is convinced of its intellectual abilities. Taking consciousness concepts from the causal, the ego will provide for the mind an endless creation of duties that range from restating old information in a new way to reevaluating an inner experience on the astral. The mind that has been touched by the energy of love generated by Soul in times of stress and decision making, will respond to the Light and Sound that can be calibrated to aid in its processes.

Babaji

How the Universal Consciousness utilizes the mind to create what we consider real in the lower worlds

The universal mind is affected by what is taking place as the Light and Sound is moved into closer proximity to the lower world and is recalibrated to be of use to the inner workings of the lower consciousness. That which was accepted in the consciousness of the whole, which is influenced and maintained in karmic balance by Kal Niranjan, is also being re-calibrated by the change of consciousness caused by the recent release of many tormented souls held in fear by some Lords of Darkness who had taken advantage of the recalibrations. What is now beginning to occur can be seen in the actions of world governments, the intolerance from a lack of understanding between philosophies and religion, and how people are set against each other in the name of God.

As all ways of life are being infused with the new Light and Sound, the warring faction will increasingly find it impossible to affect the universal consciousness in the way it had been doing in the passing dark times of the outer manifestation of the consciousness of this planet. You can visibly see this reality being affected by the infectious spread of the higher frequencies of love that are being generated through the new Light and Sound. The new Light and Sound is being anchored here through many vortices that originate from great power sources far outside this universe on planes of a much higher consciousness than have ever been constructed before. The cross-dimensional influences also lend to the job of rebalancing the universal consciousness to bring it more in line with the renaissance of love taking place. The universal consciousness has followed in the pattern of the overwhelming belief in a great destruction which must happen before a new rebirth, but the Light and Sound that is emanating from the heart of this mighty Sugmad is changing the process of renewal in this cosmos.

The Beginning Has No End

How the mind can create and uncreate what we understand as reality

In its limited environment, the energy of the mind, when it uses its access to the Light and Sound, will generate a change in the physical manifestation of its surroundings. The mind merely perceives the circumstances of its environment, analyzes it, and draws a conclusion called reality. So as it grows closer to the energy of Soul (as the mental body and Soul work closer together in manifesting the love in your daily lives), the mind will take every opportunity to recreate its perception of what the inner bodies are responding to, based on the heart energy that is being communicated from Soul. That is why one day a set of circumstances will be wonderful, and the next day the mind will question it. As you continue to practice your spiritual exercises to help the mind's clarity vibrate closer to the bandwidth of the higher consciousness of Soul, it will lose its interest in its small perceptions called "reality" and acquiesce to that of the higher consciousness working through the heart from the directives of Soul, which is in constant contact with the love of Sugmad.

Why the mind works like a machine to be continually directed by Soul

The awareness of being is governed by Soul's sight through the heart. The mind takes its question from ego and the mental body's limited understanding of the information brought to it by the etheric from Soul's brief examples of the God power in use in daily life. The mind is patterned to respond almost without forethought, and, as with any machine, if you give it fuel it runs. The fuel of the mind is information which comes from all the receptors of the outer corporeal body (the five senses). Additionally, information sometimes comes to the mind through the sixth sense resulting from the emerging awareness of Soul, and mind's increase in its limited understanding of the inner bodies' consciousnesses that affect the corresponding inner body centers of the outer senses.

The mind tends to run on these evaluations until Soul, speaking through the heart, gains its attention (usually through the emotional body) with a surge of overwhelming love and spiritual attention. Like any other machine, mind can be cared for and given regular maintenance so that it can run in good order. In this case, the spiritual exercises will keep the mind connected to its higher responsibility, that of communicating with the heart on all matters that affect its surroundings.

How God seekers can prevent others from manipulating the operation and processes of their thoughts

During or after your morning contemplation, tune the mind to its highest aspect of being via the heart connection to Soul, and provide the mind with the knowledge that only those things in accordance with the highest state of caring will influence its processes for the day.

As always, maintain an open sacred heart to the love of Sugmad for Soul; its involvement in the manifest life of the true God seeker will lead to the vibratory protection that the Living Master is sworn to, in his duty as we work together in the re-organization of this universe and its energy structure. When the mind operates from a strong sense of self, it can provide a defense from thoughts of invading entities that would guide it into destructive attitudes. The daily interplay in the manifest reality can leave the mind open to invasion by unwanted images that can be cast off by the emotional bodies of those in fear. But this, too, can be protected against with close adherence to the spiritual exercises that have been made available to address these things as you travel in the world of duality and illusion.

How love is a natural perceptual filter for the mind, and a natural defense from those whose paths are other than the Middle Way

The Beginning Has No End

Love sets the vibration of all that we encounter. Whenever the need to find an answer to that which may perplex you arises, the source of great wisdom can always be accessed through the open selfless heart which has a direct channel to the highest source of the love of Sugmad. The practice of detachment and detached goodwill sets up the environment that we walk through each day. Once the heart has set in place the vibration of Soul into your lower consciousness, it will guide you through the daily activities, and act as a warning device as to when an encroachment is taking place on the sacred ground of the selfless heart, guarded by the ever-watchful eye of Sugmad.

Babaji

Technique I: A contemplative technique that will assist the God seeker in disciplining the mind

To bring the mind back from its wandering, takes a simple focusing technique each day to create the discipline necessary to keep a clear singleness of purpose. The **HU** is the greatest multi-purpose focusing mantra. Sing the **HU** <u>five times,</u> then settle into a brief contemplation and direct the mind to perform the duties of the day without concern to danger or mishap. Assure it of its protection by the love of the Inner Master.

Technique II: A contemplative technique that filters out negativity embedded in the mind

An exercise was given to discover the negative engrams that interrupt the progress of the participant who seeks to move toward the God Worlds. This mantra is a shorter form that is specifically tuned for the mind's negativity. This is best used when a negative thought occurs during your day that must be removed.

NUM-SAT-HA-YATA

If used in the morning contemplation, this mantra can be set in place to activate when the heart senses the mind sliding toward negative thoughts.

Technique III: A contemplative technique that protects the God seeker from the throes of practitioners of the right and left hand paths

Those that seek to disrupt the focus of the God seeker's resolve usually bring a disturbance into the energy field of the mind. Found here is a Buddhist mantra for peace, which is the best defense against a disturbance.

OHM-SHAANTI-SHAANTI

Chapter 11

The Eyes of Soul

To see with the eyes of Soul, one must be willing to see as far as forever stretches and as deep as the infinite wisdom of God.

The Beginning Has No End

Seeing with the Eyes of Soul

One must understand the process of sight to gain the great rewards from seeing through the Eyes of Soul. To see is to receive input from a source of illumination or reflection that is then translated into useable information. To see with the eyes of Soul, one must be willing to see as far as forever stretches and as deep as the infinite wisdom of God. What the Soul sees is the fabric of truth made manifest by love. This love is the communication of the Light and Sound reaching to the hearts of true seekers of God Awareness. To accept the ability to understand what you see as Soul is to completely release all attachments to that which your outer senses define as reality. If Soul is the true self that we awaken to, then the God Realms, our true home, will bring new vision of wonders and vibration unknown to the newly emerging consciousness of your higher beingness. You must prepare your inner self for the new understandings that are transmitted via the Light and Sound at its highest frequency in the wisdom temples of the hierarchy, and in messages from the hearts of the Masters as they take you along the path of your Mastership. Open your heart to a different way of understanding the variances in the vibratory range of being that come through the eyes of Soul. Know that within your heart is the ability to transform this new vision to see into the usable vibrations of wisdom that the Light and Sound carry. Seeing with these eyes is not unlike being held in the arms of infinite light.

This vision can be applied to your day-to-day experiences in the lower realms of being. As said, your heart will translate all that you see with the eyes of Soul. So be aware that you shall see, in all of these realms of being, a new compassion for those who have a place within themselves for the Initiate of the Light and Sound. The range of this vision in the manifest reality can vary according to the level of selflessness that you have aspired to in your own spiritual quest to be one with the desires of this universe, held in the heart of Sugmad. As you awaken to this ability to see, know that with it comes an increase in the frequency of knowledge that flows through your consciousness and that its use is for the giving of Divine Love from the heart of Sugmad to all that you encounter.

Why Masters say that Soul's perception is 360 degrees

The perception of Soul is all-encompassing, which is to say that it is spherical. Seeing in terms of Soul is the overall awareness of being, and as we exist in truth, in forever, we may perceive it as truly infinite. The vision of Soul can answer questions about those sages that you may pass during a Universal Soul Movement or when meeting a species from another dimension for the first time,. Through Soul, you may be able to recognize the energy in which the Masters appear in this temporal time matrix. The energetic act of seeing through Soul brings the wisdom of heart-to-heart exchange to new levels of knowledge available to you as Soul. As you venture into this area of beingness and gain this vision, be prepared for more changes to the spiritual structure of the inner body alignment.

As you move to higher states of knowledge and the true use of wisdom, the knowledge that exists on a sub-atomic level becomes unveiled to you and you will begin to actually breathe in this knowledge. As you use the pure God substance more and more in your perception, the limitless process of knowingness that you have accepted into your true heart in Soul will become very apparent to you.

The non-gender aspect of Soul and why the physical form of the Masters on the Inner is a matter of choice

Some may wonder about the identity of their selfless beingness and how to be able to recognize other souls when traveling in the Inner Realms. All souls have a specific polarity of vibration, which is translated through the Eyes of Soul into what we call "color" in the manifest world. Each exudes a very highly charged presence when released from the temporal boundaries, and in our selflessness is imbedded the all-knowingness that comes with Mastership. Simply said, we all know each other as ourselves. As Soul travels in a veil of Light and Sound along the corridors of love, we may relate to those souls that we encounter according to what the mental body sends across the etheric to soothe its need to understand. That is why we may need to see Soul with gender even though in the realms above the Great Divide all exists as a vibratory frequency of Sugmad's love.

The Masters may appear with gender when the wisdom that is being carried to you heart-to-heart is placed in reference to other inner bodies for acceptance into your karmic contract and duties to Sugmad. Their actual appearance has been represented in many ways and that's just in this universe. Be wise to know that if you have been selected by a Master to be mentored in a specific area of beingness, they will present themselves to you to bring to your heart the desire to journey wherever it is you need to travel to gain wisdom and bring you to your Mastership. So if in your journey you begin to lose sight of gender, know that you are walking hand-in-hand with a Master with great love for you, and you may choose to see what pleases the sight of your soul.

How the God seeker can access the information of Soul on a daily basis, and why some Masters call Soul a historical document

The open heart transmits messages from the upper realms to those that have use of the knowledge and wisdom for the daily duty to Sugmad's love. It is in the morning contemplation that the connection is made, and throughout the day the use of mantras and brief moments of conscious contact with the love that passes through you brings the Light and Sound into focus and delivers whatever the Overseers have prepared for your daily growth. Over time, Soul has been accessed by the Lords of Karma and through many lifetimes it has progressed to this time of change. The vast experience of Soul's journey is imprinted upon the scrolls of its records and within the spiritual cells that are reproduced each time Soul once again decides to make the journey through the cycle of beingness. God-Realization within this cycle will bring this Sugmad to the new understanding that is represented in the manifestation of the Sehaji Order below, in the manifest form of beingness that we have shared over many hundreds of years. The change that has been produced and is coming into complete cosmic balance is being brought about by the participants in The Way of Truth who are bringing the greatest joy ever manifested in all realms at once. All ages that have passed are finally at rest and what is to transpire is their beginning that has no end. We shall, as timeless Masters of the Sea of Love and Mercy, exist in the infinite love of God, forever.

How the Lords of Karma and the spiritual hierarchies influence the reincarnations cycle of Soul

In the time before the first beginning there was an interval that appears as an end, but in truth was the non-time in which the Lords of Karma and the spiritual hierarchy would re-design the Sugmad to bring forth the greatest love conceivable to the manifest mind that was passing through the cycle. As of this time, all souls in existence have been constructed of the purest fabric designed from the God substance. It is infused with the Light and Sound and a fire of knowledge that shall burn forever until all souls in this cycle are consumed into God Consciousness, marked by the complete blending of all into the center of Sugmad's heart of creation and beingness. This grand journey of wisdom and experience has brought to fruition the manifestation of Sugmad in the higher realms, and for this time of change it is being brought below the Great Divide to blend all into the one expression of love that is the ultimate expression of the God-Realized state of oneness that is this Sugmad. All the karmic scrolls and records from the time since Kusulu's formation of the Red Dragon Order are planned, at this time, to reach the balance once designed by that which has non-existence, that which shall never be, but has always been Sugmad.

The Beginning Has No End

All the souls that make up this moment have been carried through their cycles based upon the needs of This One to reveal Its True Self. Once It has gazed upon Itself, It will know the peace that has been Its search since the beginning. In all the karma that has passed, the time of complete release into the middle existence, that of non-existence, transpires in the hearts of this Sugmad's Great Souls.

Why the seeker's soul agreement with life takes precedence over freewill

At this time of evolvement taking place, the souls who inhabit this Sugmad's universe have been granted the joy of freewill. One effect of this freedom has been the strengthening of life contracts. Since the great plan for this Sugmad is to bring all souls to the God Realms of consciousness, each Soul traveling through the human cycle of beingness has been given a life contract that requires an open selfless heart so that those souls who have been caught in the illusion can be awakened to come and join in the return home. So as you of The Way of Truth are the warriors sent forth to blaze the trail and search for those souls that will be brought to full consciousness through the transmission of the Light and Sound in its new frequency, your life contracts have been placed in the priority of the Grand Council for instant review. The desire is to continually maintain the delicate balance of the cosmic forces that have been raised in variance to aid this transition of souls. As each of you can choose a direction, it will always become aligned with the greater mission of this Sugmad to awaken the slumbering souls and release all souls that may suffer in the illusion or who may be caught in the battle in the world of duality between the seemingly dark forces who apply karma and the forces of light that balance that karma, but all of which have work to do for this time of love spreading throughout this Sugmad.

Babaji

Questions for Babaji – I

How did you physically manifest yourself before the following saints: Lahiri Mahasaya who was Sri Yukteswar's teacher; Sri Shankara (788-820 A.D.) and the poet Kabir (1398-1448 A.D.)?

How and why were these men initiated by you into the Kriya Yoga tradition?

As Lahiri was walking beside the river, I sat beneath a tree and appeared as a perplexed, somewhat lost, soul. At that time he was in search of his Master, and I had seen in his heart the sorrow for the coming time that would stress the spiritual energy in this universe. Since he was already being filled with the love of God through the Light and Sound, he relieved himself of his own woes to console me. It was at this time that I filled his heart with the message of undying devotion to understanding that love is always the key that releases the Soul to join with God while existing in troubled times of spiritual chaos. We sat for hours as I asked him questions of the heart and how I should go about releasing the supposed woes of life to once again fill my heart with joy. As we finished our conversation he rose to his feet and thanked me. He recognized my mantle and expressed gratitude for the blessing; he knew of his mission to teach those things that we had discovered together.

As for the poet Kabir, whose mind was drenched in the glory of cosmic enlightenment and could channel the purest of God's heart through his poetry, I knew that debate was his path to the Light and Sound he found within, when he released himself to his heart. As we sat and sipped tea, and we began to examine the complexities of Soul together, I reached from my heart toward his to bring a gentle rest to his search. He then reached out and touched my hand and asked me if I could offer him guidance to understand completely the great love that filled his heart. As I introduced the Light and Sound to him and spoke of how love was the language through which the Soul truly speaks, he seemed to lift from the mental entanglement and his heart cleared. At that time he recognized my mantle and offered his thanks. Once again the message of love, devotion and caring was set in place to become a part of this spiritual time of beginning. As he walked away, I had a sense in my heart that I had placed a gift into the hands that would share this with many souls seeking the same understanding.

Babaji

Questions for Babaji – II

How did you mentor Jesus Christ between the ages of 12-30? Elaborate on what areas of spirituality you taught him. After the teachings were finished, was he aware that his mission would be short-lived?

Christ was inquisitive and had already understood that his mission was of great importance. At the time, he traveled to distant lands in search of wisdom. We met on the inner planes as his powers of contemplation were well-focused upon the many answers that he would find in his consciousness as he was drawn toward his duty to the Light and Sound that filled his heart. We discussed the question of reaching souls that seemed uninterested in their salvation. I gave to him the need to bring forth from people's hearts the desire to love one another without judgment or expectation. We talked of the need to reach those who had taken the Light and Sound and constricted its movement and how to once again let it reach those lost in the illusion of pain and suffering. He confided in me that for some reason he already understood the idea of great suffering. He understood that part of his mission would be to bear the suffering of all souls that would find in him salvation from those things that clouded their hearts and prevented the light of God from shining through. It was at this time that the realization of the quick end of his life was made clear to us both. As his life progressed he would return to me in contemplation to gain strength when he felt that his frailties would place his heart in jeopardy and he would lose the path of his mission. I reassured him that God our Father was watching over us all and his plan was complete and that many would be given access to the Light and Sound through his teaching for hundreds of years.

The Beginning Has No End

Questions for Babaji - III

What was your relationship with Milarepa, the great Tibetan Sage between the 11th and 12th centuries? What was the nature and content of the dialogue that was exchanged between the two of you?

Milarepa was a great soul. I was brought to his heart in contemplation and we discussed things of a worldly nature, for he who had left this behind had many questions about how this would affect the wisdom that he had attained. It was my place, as the carrier of the Light and Sound, to bring to his heart that his understanding of suffering was something that in this time would bring a great balance to the heart of the One who is the Guardian of Creation. He asked me the reason for my place in the spiritual realms and I confided in him that I was chosen from among a great many souls to travel through the temporal existence to bring the message of love that is felt in all hearts that have suffered, and that each and every Soul carries the joy of the higher realms of realization, and that his sacrifice for the sake of manifesting the Light and Sound would give him the place as the head of The Grand Council of Sugmad's hierarchy. In this time he would see all of the souls that looked to his great devotion as a guiding light to truth at all costs and that it would be truth that would be their salvation – truth of love and devotion. His addition to the karmic scrolls of the great Overseer has proven to set the initiation process into an order that allows only those devoted to the purity of heart to have the key to navigating the higher realms successfully. He gave to me the insight that all hearts deserve to be filled with the Light and Sound, and that all forgiveness is the greatest in vibrations in the frequencies of love as he practices today in matters of cosmic karma.

137

Babaji

How God seekers can speak to others as Soul

As a God seeker, it has become a part of your soul contract to talk with all souls that approach you in search of their connection to the Light and Sound. That is why Dan Rin has taken you to this new level of universal consciousness - to be able to walk in the God Worlds and to be trained in the use of the God power through the selfless sacred heart transmission of the Masters as you walk in the realms below the Great Divide. This grand experiment is to bring the Light and Sound to all souls and to have them join in the joy of this Sugmad and to raise the spiritual awareness to the levels of God-Realization for all open-hearted travelers. This is the reason you are being trained as Sehaji Masters to walk amongst all beings of this universe and give the love of Sugmad to waiting, open hearts.

The Beginning Has No End

A contemplative exercise that will enable the practitioner to listen to the direction of their own Soul

Settle into the quietude of contemplation with the **HU** song and your sacred word.

Bring your focus on the Eyes of Soul looking into the heart of Sugmad and see the swirl of colors that are its vibrations of love.

There will be some of these colors that will harmonically resonate within your heart center.

As you come out of contemplation, take pen and paper and write the question:

What is my direction as Soul today?

Use the mantra **MUTA-PARUM** spoken <u>three times</u> slowly; this will translate the pure transmissions of love into useable directions as you begin to write.

Babaji

Chapter 12

Living with Heart

To hear the instructions that are given to you moment-by-moment, the stillness of the heart must be maintained at all times.

The Beginning Has No End

What it means to live this life and beyond with Heart

Heart is the communication essence of our true beingness in Soul. The heart is the point from which we can experience the richness of life given by the flow of the Light and Sound in this corporeal life and our spiritual existence and all our soul growth and beyond, when we translate to oneness in the essence of love within the Sea of Love and Mercy. In this human life, the heart is an extremely vital mode of understanding to bring the grace of love to all things that we travel through in this journey of Soul. In daily life as we pass through situations that affect our inner alignment of being, the heart will provide an answer that is charged with the Light and Sound. We may not be able to hear the subtle message of love that resolves all things that are a part of being human. Corporeal things are usually examined by the mental and emotional bodies, and with the limited understanding from the ego, we respond to our environment with this information which may not be charged with the Light and Sound. It may be merely a response set forth by old engrammatic residue that shows in this plane of experience.

The presence of God is always with you of the Sacred Heart consciousness; it is just a matter of connecting to it. Enlisting the flow of the heart energy into these things will bring a greater sense of connection to the presence of God in the day-to-day exchanges of our lower consciousness. These things perplex God seekers less and less as they navigate through the mire of this corporeal life less, as they learn to allow the higher aspects of the love of Sugmad to be more and more present in the things that they say and do. It is the journey of Soul through the human life process that enriches the quality and quantity of heart energy, and charges our existence in this and higher realms. To gain the wisdom from Sugmad, that which has placed us here in Its effort to bring love to Itself, enriches every moment of this journey filled with opportunity to bring the higher aspects of beingness into alignment with our evolution toward the God Worlds.

Babaji

To have the focus of life be of pure heart, is to bring a quality to this existence that will always maintain the delicate cosmic balance, and will allow this Sugmad to grow in the next generation of spiritual beings that we are to become - a generation wherein all of our actions are charged with the Light and Sound manifested in new ways of awareness. Once these things have come to pass, those that follow will bring a new generation of light-beings that will replace this existence that we call corporeal with that of the pure essence of beingness, and will allow those of other genetic make-up to once again be part of this reality. These things have been in existence before and were lost when the direction of the Light and Sound was diverted by the ego-driven gains of those that caused the destruction of the great continents of Lemuria and Atlantis.

Caring, one of the great qualities of the selfless open heart, is how the Light and Sound is now blended into the acts of those who truly search for ways to make the presence of God felt in their daily lives. After all, is it not the wish of this Sugmad to have Its love felt in every consciousness that It has brought into creation? Be well advised to learn the lesson given by the Lords of Karma in these experiences in the lower realms, so that you may understand that the way of the selfless heart is the way that this great love that fuels the universe can be shared between all that would be one with their God essence through the heart.

Why the heart consciousness is the only facet of our physical body we can take into the God Worlds

Our higher selves respond to the vibration of communication that is best described by the word "love". Know that, of the words that have been charged with the Light and Sound and create within every individual the desire to be God-Realized, "love" is the one that not only carries the Light and Sound in its vibration, but also can intensify the heart of the seeker who truly opens himself to its full potential. As for our humanness, which is what we are taking to its greatest manifestation in this Sugmad, it has the ability to assimilate this communication into the lower realms while still holding the deeper essence of God's original purpose - that is, creating the experience for Soul to learn of itself as part of God's manifestation in this universe. While in the human experience, Soul can access the God power only through the portal of the open selfless heart center of the physical form, for it is the most accessible of the inner energy centers that correspond to the cosmic structure of Sugmad's body. It is the harmonic resonance that can be felt and seen in the astral and etheric planes when the heart of a true seeker is opened for the first time, and it is at this time that the first infusion of the Light and Sound reaches the emerging soul of the seeker of God-Realization. The product of this process is manifestation of the greatest quantities of love that the lower shell can maintain while the consciousness is focused on the higher self. The resulting alignment allows the higher consciousness to be present within the upper harmonic variances in the lower consciousness which allow access to a limited use of knowledge housed in the great wisdom temples of the God planes.

If the selfless heart energy of being becomes a conduit for the lower needs of our humanness, it will be able to pass through the heart center of the corporeal shell into the flow of activities of your aware soul that guides you through daily life. The quality of the heart that can cross into the consciousness of being of the God Worlds is achieved when seekers are truly willing to allow themselves to become completely transparent: being of no ego, existing in the highest form of detached goodwill, and seeking through the God power to be of service to this Sugmad to complete Its mission in all vibratory levels of understanding.

There is so much more that is available through the effort of the heart to aid Soul in its karmic duty - namely, the duty of manifesting the effect of the God Worlds, via the Light and Sound, so that those hearts that stand in readiness can join with all those who have allowed the presence of God to guide them from the ignorance that has so long kept them from their true purpose of love in this universe. Place your true self in the pure essence of love and see that the grace of Sugmad's love will heal all things from before and beyond now.

How you learn to apply the heart consciousness to all of your life decisions

We have touched on the giving of detached goodwill toward all things, and have said much of the transparent quality of heart necessary to let the light of God's love shine into all places where our consciousness operates. To take this ability and use its highest purpose is to see its place in all of your affairs. This is the wisdom that is accessible when the heart is focused on the middle path of non-power when moving in any realm of experience. The presence of heart is to allow the Light and Sound to carry the love of Sugmad into all corners of your movement in the lower experiences of being, those of the temporal world of perception. It is this linear sense of processing the day-to-day activities that can be brought into alignment with the higher source of guidance available through the heart consciousness. The heart consciousness aligns itself with frequencies of the Light and Sound for specific use in the worlds of decision making that is governed by the mental body's activity. As said before, once the mental body has been guided to a better understanding of the use of heart energy in its processes, the ability of the mind, in its day-to-day use, will be enhanced by the presence of the transmutable frequencies of wisdom and understanding that are being carried in transmission across the Great Divide in the Light and Sound of today.

Life is a part of Sugmad's love manifested and is absorbed by the pure energy of the heart that is connected to the God Worlds through Universal Soul Movement. The wisdom that is focused through the process of reflection in these journeys is infused into the consciousness of Soul. This wisdom can then be accessed by the mental body to aid the mind in making its decisions without the influence of the causal and emotional bodies which tend to draw the mind off course with old karmic and engrammatic information. When you encounter a situation that presents you with a feeling of less control, this is a time when you may be put into the process of channeling this stored information. This information is released into useable form directly through the focusing power of the heart that has been placed into the non-power mode of detachment. The release from wants and needs brings to the mental body the awareness of the presence of the love that provides the wisdom of the higher realms to be utilized in all forms of awareness.

The heart is the most sensitive instrument for accessing the many levels of understanding of knowledge that are provided to Soul for use in its travels through all realms of experience that are made available for growth toward its highest goals and aspirations within its effort to spread the love of Sugmad.

How we, as God seekers, can measure the true intent of another's heart

Once again, we must be aware that we are a part of Soul's karmic path of advancement towards the God-Realized state of being. The Lords of Karma will present to us, via the conduit of the open, sacred heart, those things that will bring maximum benefit to our journey with good spiritual guidance and understanding. It can never be expressed too often, to those of us who seek to bring the God Consciousness into focus in this universe, that caring is the greatest effort that produces the strongest results in terms of dispensing the Divine Love of Sugmad. Those who approach with uncertain intent can be guided to us by the presence of balance that is yours through the non-power focus of a selfless heart. The heart is that which can examine those who come to us along the path to perhaps bring us through an experience that the Lords of Karma have prescribed to better prepare us for Mastership. It is the heart that can decipher the vibration of the exchange that is taking place. Use the tools of the sacred heart: detachment, selfless understanding of God's guidance of Soul, and always seeking the highest level of Sugmad's love in the consciousness of others.

Once the practice of selfless caring is focused on the karmic path of the seeker, our only encounters will be those of a nature to bring more knowledge, wisdom and a greater capacity to love. Your choice to seek Mastership requires of you the desire to seek the highest vibration of selflessness to better reflect and give understanding to all circumstances in this universe that may come to bear upon your evolution toward true God-Realization.

How we can keep our heart connected to Sugmad's heart consciousness

As Soul grows in its endless journey in the God Worlds, there is created within it a need to be fulfilled with the accomplishment of understanding the knowledge and wisdom that is shared by the Masters. The guidance that it requires comes from the heart of Sugmad. This builds into the inner awareness of the seeker the desire to be in conscious contact with that which it knows is its eternal breath of life – the heart of Sugmad. Again and again this brings us to the subject of the selfless heart and its ability to act in a detached mode of caring, that of the God power, the middle path. This is where Soul can remain in a connective mode of understanding to that which is its guide, and it is through heart-to-heart communication that Sugmad will avail Itself. The act of devotion, which is one of the highest forms of caring, will always guide the pure of heart to the place of acceptance in the center of Sugmad's heart.

The guidance gained from this effort on the part of the participants in The Way of Truth is one of the pillars of stability that is built by compassion and caring for the conscious contact with the center of beingness in the heart of Sugmad. We all need to aspire to this lofty, seemingly unattainable aspect of our awareness that is easily accomplished through the simplest of efforts – that of the loving heart consciousness that shines through the transparent selflessness of those who seek to walk as Masters of total beingness in all realms.

Why we must maintain the heart of a spiritual warrior in our daily affairs

Within the world of our daily lives we must carry the love of Sugmad to be the light that will guide those yet in darkness and those that still slumber, so that they may be awakened to the love that has infused this universe with a great new hope. It is the hope that soon the spiritual hierarchies of this Sugmad will make themselves known in an embodiment below the Great Divide, and to present a great relief to the age-old beliefs of karmic cycling. The new Light and Sound carries in it the wisdom that is transmitted to the open hearts of those who have taken up this mission of recalibrating the spiritual energy of this and many other universes. As we carry the mighty sword of Sugmad's love and compassion for all souls at all levels of awareness, we strike with caring at those who still choose to suffer in the illusion of duality. We vigilantly move forward so that they may be awakened to the unwavering force and healing energy of the universal love that we of the God-Realized consciousness are carrying to them. This love is a great brilliance emanating from the Light and Sound that shines through the transparent selflessness that our open hearts are prepared to share with those that choose to be awakened to the might and graces of this loving force. We travel together as warriors in Sugmad's armies of compassion and love with the help of the Great Ones – past, present and future – to bring the Light and Love back to the center of beingness in all realms.

We must maintain the vigilance of well-trained warriors and move with confidence in the great love that we wield through the execution of detached well-being to all that we encounter on this journey that has no end.

Babaji

How the heart consciousness is the transmitter for our spiritual conversations with the Sehaji

As the Sehaji tutor you on your journey to becoming one and the same as they, their instructions are exact and must be followed. Variances will come from the adjustments made by the Lords of Karma who may choose to accelerate your progress when tremendous acts of selfless caring are shown in each day of your life. To hear the instructions that are given to you moment-by-moment, the stillness of the heart must be maintained at all times. If you allow your heart to remain open to these transmissions, the wealth of knowledge that is stored in the collective consciousnesses of those who are timeless Masters will always be available to your consciousness. The moment you are willing to be one with the wishes of this Sugmad in the reformation of the greatest of spiritual realms, and you stand before the tasks that are a part of the karmic duties of those of The Way of Truth, the wisdom to carry them out is instantaneous. It is only through the focus of the heart that the detailed knowledge can be delivered to all levels of awareness. And through this connection, the questions that may bring pause to the effort toward your own Mastership can be answered, even before your awareness has formulated their contents. The Sehaji have dedicated themselves to your guidance and watch you as the acceleration of the change is supported by all who take part in it. I continue to be of complete availability to all of you who seek my knowledge and wisdom as you move through the lower realms carrying this great consciousness that has been bestowed upon you.

How we can purge our hearts of negative engrams through acts of love and forgiveness

Those acts of less-than-perfect intentions that may have been potentially listed in your karmic scrolls can be adjusted as you grow in the abilities of the selfless heart to act from detached goodwill and motivate the God power from the center path of non-

150

power. When you choose to take the path of love and forgiveness when confronted by these potential intentions, the karmic scrolls are adjusted accordingly.

The Light and Sound grows in strength as you continue to practice acts of love and caring. Look not for greatness in these things, but for the most unnoticed aspects of your open heart. The acts of your daily life may weigh heavily in the judgment of the Lords of Karma and in the requests made by the Sehaji, so be mindful of your inner alignment with the love and caring that has been your guide to bring you to this beginning, and marks the point at which you may embark on your travels through the higher realms of beingness offered to you.

As the Light and Sound grows in strength within you, the new polarity that it brings to your inner bodies will begin to purge negative engrams relative to the use of selflessness in all areas of your daily life. As you practice the virtues of selflessness, the engrams of negativity can no longer exist in such a strong environment of love and caring. These engrams usually relate to those moments of weakness and doubt that may briefly be felt as the mental body struggles with its new awareness that the heart is guiding its duties. This may give rise to an emotional body overload which will create in the causal, the embryo of a negative engram that will naturally be stored by the mind to affect its purpose. But once returned to the higher aspects of all inner workings, these embryos and subsequent engrams will be purged by the selflessness that guides your true nature.

How God seekers can influence the hearts of others without intrusion upon their space and freedom

When the presence of the Light and Sound is felt by one of lesser awareness, their inner self will respond to the change in the spiritual vibration of the moment. If, as a true selfless soul, you stand without notice, this person will walk away with a new sense that somewhere, somehow, there has been a change to their awareness. This is one of the great effects that you, as a heightened soul, have upon your surroundings. Those who spend time with you will begin to notice that they have a need for a greater understanding of what they are starting to awaken to within themselves. The grace of Sugmad, transmitted through the Light and Sound that you carry in your heart, washes over those who have the smallest of cracks appearing in their consciousness. The grace that is combined in the effort of your true self to connect to the highest wishes of Sugmad is the greatest, most energetic change that many may encounter before their complete awakening takes place. Know in yourself that this is not an intrusion, but is like letting someone, for the first time, take a deep breath of clear, fresh air, or is like drawing back the veil and allowing to be shown, in a new brilliance, that which had not been conceived by the slumbering consciousness of this soul. Only in acts of less-than-caring will this action jolt someone and cause a moment of discomfort. This usually happens if there is some sort of karmic interplay that was not written into either of your life contracts, but was the result of some combined actions in another lifetime between your higher aspects of being which, until this time, was not yet activated. There are fewer and fewer incidents of this kind because the purging of many engrams left by the Dark Lords have all but disappeared from the karmic path of the newly liberated souls of this earth.

Be wise to the fact that you carry the grace of the God power that affects the temporal systems of those of lesser awareness, and that only the love that governs your every action tempers the effect that can occur. To learn the true meaning of detached goodwill can end these unforeseen possibilities as you progress along the path of God-Realization manifested.

The Beginning Has No End

Herein is a contemplative exercise that can place us in the highest aspect of the heart consciousness in our daily communications at work, with family and at play

Each morning you must start with the acquisition of Sugmad's highest grace and place that within the center of your heart beingness.

After a ten-minute **HU** song, state out loud:

I operate through the heart consciousness of Sugmad.

<u>Do this three times</u>.

The reactivation mantra that you can use during your day is:

TRESTE-TU-MASTE

Or you may simply repeat the affirmation in a quiet moment of your day.

Babaji

Chapter 13

The True Nature of Balance In the Universe

*Love is the undisturbed balance
that binds this universe together.*

The Beginning Has No End

The True Nature of Balance in the Universe

In the crucible of nothingness from which all creation was born, there was added a formula of measurement that produced a perfect balance at the epoch of this moment called the universe. When this all began, it was set forth in perfect balance and contained no right or wrong, no left or right, no up or down – a true, perfect balance. As the Creator examined Its handiwork, It set forth the process of experience within Its heart to bring life into Its being. As this life was born of the same balance as the Eternal Being, it existed in harmony with its creator. The experiences of self became part of the travels of consciousness that grew from self-awareness, those items of the dual nature of existence in perfect balance. As the simultaneous levels of beingness grew within themselves, variations of expression took on a life of seeming chaos, but all remained in balance. Time began and the multiple stages of awareness caused the first imbalance that was presented when thought set forth to define its own beginnings in an environment where it could not exist. In this creativity was born the universal ego that has since permeated the consciousness of the beginning, and created the imbalance that exists in the mirror of life, the illusion that our consciousness suffers through as it is born into the journey of soul.

Time is the measure of existence to the balance of the cosmic energy that lights the universe. Through the many cycles of soul's existence, there has been held an imbalance and it has caused what Soul experiences as karma. As Sugmads across all existence began to feel the love that had brought about this beginning, and the subsequent chaos of imbalance, a hierarchy of beings was created to seek a balance of love - the original purpose of the beginning. Soul has passed through many permutations of vibratory expressions of its oneness and has struggled through the lies that it has been told by the variant energies of karmic confusion; consciousness has been split by two equal karmic choices. This effort to bring balance has allowed the dual entities of dark and

157

light to exist side-by-side. The vastness of this universe's creation could not be comprehended until it expanded itself into worlds of duality, thus the light and darkness became a place of learning.

The search for balance is drawing to it the point of the new beginning of the awakening of the great return of this universe to its true self – that of love. Souls from every area of beingness have begun to see or sense this. Through the haze of confusion, that of the etheric, the light of the original being is now seen. The original creation of balance that had been stopped on the circular cycle of the dual belief of balance and rebirth is reforming in the higher consciousness of being. The great love that fills the heart of creation is magnified through the Sugmads of each existence that fills this universe. At this time in the return of love, the balance of souls that have grown to Mastership in all levels of consciousness has synthesized the vibration of love into forms of wisdom that are passed to levels of realities that many souls live in and bring a guidance from the original heart of creation. With the might of the Light and Sound carrying this energetic stream of God substance to all of existence, the beginning that has no end has taken its place, and draws all to see the pure balance that never left but has only been covered by the experience of Soul to know its true self within the heart of creation – that of perfect balance in love.

Beneath the multiple levels of consciousness – that of the physical, astral, causal, mental, etheric and spiritual – the true harmony of love is a single tone. It sets up the resonance of wisdom and aligns all the pathways for awareness for Soul to travel along so that it may reach, once again, its ultimate unification with the Light and Sound. This vibration existed before time set forth the mesh of misguided efforts to re-unify that which has always been one within itself, and is now brought back to its original state of expression through the long cycle of the journey of Soul. Love is the undisturbed balance that binds this universe together.

Chapter 14

What is Your Place of Understanding?

We all travel through the adventures of life many times until we have reached the understanding that what we bring back to the central pool of creation adds tothe universal knowledge shared between all Sugmads and all creations.

The Beginning Has No End

Preparations that Soul receives before it chooses the body for its next incarnation

It is within the attitude of karma that Soul is prepared for each journey it takes through Sugmad for its quest of understanding the selfless nature of its existence. As the Lords of Karma have watched over this process from each beginning of each Sugmad, every Soul is guided by its past wisdom of self and purpose, to its new process of being that it must endure. The time has arrived for Soul to end its cycle on the Wheel of 84 when its first choices of bodies were made according to the will of Sugmad and Its needs to reform the true balance within Its universe. As you of The Way of Truth have been taught, there exists for each Soul a karmic duty to perform that is part of bringing balance back to this Sugmad, and to bring the process of beingness to its true beginning, which is to rest with contentment in the heart of God forever within the Sea of Love and Mercy. The corporeal shell that is presented for choice is one that grows with the journey to be able to house the cosmic force carried by the God power through the final cycle. Each one is constructed to hold the energy of the materials that have been infused with the God substance, and will allow the Soul to integrate the Light and Sound into all levels of awareness. From the beginning of all journeys, know that I have seen this process bring great change and wonder to those that have given themselves to the guidance of the Living Masters that brought this universe to its greatest effort to satisfy Sugmad.

Communications between the Lords of Karma and Soul about its next life contract

As Soul steps forward to begin its journey, once again, around the cycle of learning, the karmic scrolls are brought before the Lords of Karma and examined with care. The level of Mastership each Soul has practiced is taken into account as Soul makes its request for the levels of accomplishment it desires for the next incarnation. As all the deeds and debts are placed before Soul and it is asked

161

about the wisdom of every action taken in each encounter, it must provide an understanding that can be added to the evolutionary process of the Golden Wisdom Library. The cumulative knowledge of Sugmad is gathered by each Soul that has traveled from one side to the other of all the experiences that are available to It through Its cycle of examination. As the Lords of Karma calculate what the needs are for the continued evolvement of Sugmad, the merits of each Soul are placed in order so that it is afforded the best chance to complete the Wheel of 84 in each cycle upon which it embarks. If a special quality of Soul is desired by the Oversoul to accomplish a particular part of the continuous balancing of the energies of existence, the adjustment to Soul's contract may be granted by the Silent Ones that oversee the operations of this and many universes throughout many Sugmads.

Criteria by which the Lords of Karma render Grace to those who give selflessly to the Light and Sound

To further elaborate on the adjustments that can be made to the life contract of souls, let us speak of those that reach the higher rungs of Mastership through their selfless devotion to the love of Sugmad. Remember that all records of good and mistaken actions are a part of the past contract of every soul, for nothing transpires within creation without a purpose. If Soul has done these things in accordance with the highest laws of Sugmad, operating through the selfless heart consciousness, the offer to move to the next levels of Mastership can be written into the life contract of Soul. If any areas that are affected by ego are seen, Soul will be held to a very strict retribution cycle – one that sees that it learns through the severest of lessons that the true path to understanding and the sacred heart is through selflessness. To maximize the flow of the Light and Sound, Soul must achieve mastery of the inherent desire to appropriate self worth from acts that are given by the love of Sugmad for it to perform, and must know that all is of love – the perfect balance that brings this universe into its highest vibration.

The Beginning Has No End

Explaining the Law of Reciprocity which says that you can receive only to the proportion of your open heart

Once back in the cycle of rebirth to travel through the manifest reality to again gain the consciousness of the higher realms, it is wise to know that an open-hearted beingness in this process provides the greatest path to understanding of what you shall accomplish through this life you have been given. As I have said many times, the simple act of caring is the greatest of Sugmad's wishes. To carry within the consciousness of your selflessness, the act of giving in the smallest quantities brings remarkable results to the adjustment of the karmic scrolls. It is not to say that you will be cast out of heaven unless all your acts are of the purest intentions, but it is to say that all that transpires in this universe is in accordance with the highest laws of Sugmad, and when contingencies of freewill may cause misdirected acts of ego, greed, lust or desire, the process to balance these things within your karmic file will require many more efforts to reach the understanding that these things cloud the path and guide the inner being back to illusion, pain and suffering. The reverse is exceedingly clear - that acts of caring and giving of detached goodwill, and not letting the ego expect rewards, is the pure and balanced path of love.

How Soul makes its choices regarding family, culture, talents, personality characteristics, desires, etc.

If it is entering into an advanced level of consciousness, Soul's entry into the cycle of the manifest reality is not so much governed by the need for specific choices as to personality, characteristics, family, culture, talents, desires, etc., to best fulfill its duties to Sugmad. Those that are starting a new cycle of spiritual growth will choose the best potential aspects in the manifested reality to maximize Soul's awareness in the physical body it will occupy. The balance to Sugmad is an infinite process. As new souls are introduced to the possibilities of existence in the physical form, and as they make the extensive preparations that are necessary, a variety of possible paths are made available. Not all paths will necessarily be focused on the pursuit of balance, but there will always be at least one that is. Since Soul is infinite and only becomes finite when it has passed through its first cycle of incarnation, the chances for choice increase as it is taken through the first rung of spiritual evolution as a neophyte. In its first cycle, it must learn of the desire that is implanted within its heart to follow the will of love that is inherent in the makeup of all that exist in God's heart.

We all travel through the adventures of life many times until we have reached the understanding that what we bring back to the central pool of creation adds to the universal knowledge shared between all Sugmads and all creations. The joy of all the wonderments that come from the journey of souls is continued and evolves until we have reached the ultimate balance of being one with love within the heart of all creation. With that said, let's say that those attributes of the corporeal process are formed after the third cycle, when Soul is placed into its first levels of cosmic awareness. At this time in its evolution, it has the consciousness to be attuned to the cosmic flow of Sugmad's heart, and may begin the process of creating its place to aid in the assurance that the gift of freewill remains a part of the growth in the changing needs of the Light and Sound.

What to say to those souls who desire to be released from the Wheel of 84

For Soul to be released from the Wheel of 84, the cycle of retribution and reincarnation, it is of the utmost importance that it become completely aligned with the will of the highest laws of creation in Sugmad. If Soul brings to its cycle the love and grace of selflessness and lends that to the balance of energies in the universe that guides it to its ultimate state-of-being, then it has performed the task that creation has given to each of us as we have traveled this path toward God-Realization. We are all part of the unified love of the Light and Sound (the movement of God through the experience called life.) The task of completing the journey is left to the guidance provided by those that care for the order in creation, and we, as Soul, are offered the understanding and wisdom which is woven into the cosmic genetic fabric that we are born into. The path to Mastership and release from the Wheel is offered at any time we choose to accept the awareness of the Light and Sound of Sugmad.

How Babaji approached the resolution of his life contract, karma, and burdens

To speak of my journeys would begin a tale that has no ending. I have been placed in the heart of many, to maintain the fire of God's desire for the best to be accomplished throughout the endless joy of love – the true fabric of existence. With the guidance of those who have been here before time itself, I have taken the duties of many that have chosen to be absorbed back into the heart of beingness to forever fuel the desires of those that journey as Soul, so that all the forces that must remain aligned in this creation are held in good stead with all the hierarchies of the God Worlds. It is a great honor that is bestowed upon me by those who bring the Light and Sound to help govern and guide the teachings of existence to all seeking the wondrous paths of Godly knowledge, wisdom and love. As I watch those of you who seek out this knowledge and love, it does lighten a burden, for if having the blessing of an all-compassionate heart is a burden, then it is one that only caring allows me to bear with joy each time I see the release of a Soul from torment and brought into the light of infinite joy by those of you that labor in the world of duality for Sugmad and the Light and Sound.

Babaji

The methods we can use to break the repetition of negative cycles in our lives

In the realms below the Great Divide where the perception of positive and negative processes veil the reality of balance, the path to the uses of this knowledge is cast in with the need for the freewill to become aligned with God. Once you have learned to operate completely from the Sacred Heart beingness and let the Light and Sound flow through your complete selflessness in the manifest knowing that you are who you are - that of the God stuff, the realized and manifested love of creation - you will be filled with the wisdom that will purge from your consciousness the inability to see through the veil of illusion and accept the rightful glory that the Light and Sound gives you.

The Beginning Has No End

A simple contemplative exercise to break negative repetition

To help in this effort I offer you this simple exercise and mantra that must be practiced from now until it is finished, which you will understand as you move through your life with it living in the background of your consciousness, forever. It is that of the universal heartbeat of the cosmos.

The center of beingness is in the blue-white light that surrounds the beginning of all knowledge within the heart of creation. Settle into contemplation and allow Soul to be released to the current of the Light and Sound that flows from the Rod of Power that has been handed to your Living Master, Dan Rin. Within his trust you will be carried to the release of all negative impulses that may penetrate the shield of your endless love of Sugmad.

Within this mantra lies great power, and it in itself is a silent one that is only safe in the thoughts of the Sacred Heart.

AOTUM (ah-o-tum)

This mantra is not to be spoken out loud, but is to be held within the center of the Sacred Heart awareness always and only heard inwardly by your self alone.

Methods and techniques we can use to speak to those we love, live with, and those who are family members

If you are truly connected to someone with selfless joy and the understanding that all love flows from the heart of God, it is just a simple matter of caring that conveys whatever communication that you need to make to loved ones that are in your presence or in a far-off place. If your state of receptivity is one of centeredness and clarity, all that is shared with family and the ones you love will be of the Sacred Heart energy. You have studied long and have been availed of the wisdom of thousands of souls that have traveled

167

through every possible adventure in this universe, so know that within your grasp is the complete ability for the clarity of thought and expression you may need.

The Beginning Has No End

**A contemplative exercise that will answer the participants'
questions concerning their spiritual mission in life**

Each change in your initiation level may have an effect on the
direction of your spiritual mission in life; it is necessary to
maintain an ever vigilant awareness of the wishes of Sugmad in
your daily life to understand Its needs for you.

Sitting in contemplation every morning and clarifying the heart so
that it may receive the guidance of the Masters is the best method
that I can offer for answering this question.

The removal of ego from the actions of giving will align you with
the highest wishes of Sugmad in your daily spiritual quest. The
absence of ego makes way for the selfless nature of pure Soul to be
available in all situations that may require the presence of the Light
and Sound.

Singing the love song to God, the **HU**, inwardly <u>five times at four
hour intervals</u> is a form of nourishment to the Soul through every
day's journey.

Babaji

Chapter 15

The Universe is Our Home

We have been placed here for a specific purpose of this Sugmad, and it is best that we take as much care of it as Sugmad has chosen to take care of us.

The Beginning Has No End

The various planes of existence and life starting with the physical, astral, causal, mental and etheric

In corporeal existence, life, as we understand it, is the experience of responses governed by the five senses. It is the five senses that govern your responses to the physical reality of being. As we venture into the realms within, the experience of existence begins to broaden as the levels of awareness begin to expand. We search to understand those things that bring questions to the higher senses of the mind. As we travel to the self-awareness stage of evolution that brings us to the door of the higher levels of consciousness below the Great Divide, we understand that within this realm of awareness there exist subtle realms of being that are defined by the texture of their reality. The astral is one of the first extra-sensory contacts that we make as we begin to travel beyond the physical shell we once thought was our only existence. This may come in the form of those dreams where you feel that there is another way of seeing. You actually feel the experience perceived to be a dream that is real to the touch of this inner sense of the astral plane. The term "astral travel" is given to this sensation when we actually can see our physical body from a vantage point other than a mirror. This is described by many people as floating above their bodies as they travel to other places of awareness within this plane of experience. As some become more availed to the abilities of the psychic realms, the process of astral travel will allow them to go to various places that have a reference point to this level of consciousness - places where they will find guidance on their chosen path to seek the higher realms of being. This plane of experience begins to open the heart to the adventures of your inner self.

Some of the visions that are brought back to the waking consciousness from the astral plane are those invoked by the causal plane of existence. Here, for the first time, you may be able to apply your feelings or emotions to that which is guiding you through your life at junctures of decision-making. They respond to the cause and effect of the worlds of duality and the illusion of good and bad things happening in your corporeal life experience. This slightly higher vibration of beingness brings us closer to the conscious opening of the heart as it searches for the source of the energetic call of our true self as Soul in the higher frequencies of beingness in these realms below the Great Divide. What this awareness does for the seeker is to bring the first vibration of the Light and Sound into the self-aware being. Why do we have such a strong response to the cause and effect aspect of being as we move through this level of initiation? The answer is this - because of the journey toward the love that seems to be guiding the Soul to a starting point of some magnitude, and because of the feelings that it provokes for its awareness. We have chose to take this journey when we took the first step toward that great love that fills this universe that we have learned to understand as the beginning of creation – that of the Heart of Sugmad.

As our self-awareness brings the experiences of the astral and causal plane to the attention of mind, it sets forth activity of the mental body which we have been using in limited ways. This level of self-awareness brings to the attention of the mental body the energy it can use to express the inner existence of being that is growing. This is one of the first stages where the mental body began to accommodate the subtle vocalization of the heart consciousness calling to its true existence. At this point the inner vibratory range of experience has now begun to become attuned to the existence of the Light and Sound in its lower frequency band felt in the corporeal shell, and it begins to influence the daily actions of life. This is when the edge of self begins to see through the veil of illusion that has been described as the mist of the etheric plane that we see on the Inner as we approach the doorway to our soul consciousness just beyond the etheric awareness. Within the etheric you will find the fabric of the astral origin already constructed. Congruently, causal forms emanate creative expression that brings awareness of purpose to the mental consciousness. This is an awareness to so much more beyond the experience of this vibration of Spirit that is the opening of the heart to the song of God's love. This spiritual melody is forever being played to us through all the experiences of this life in the coarse representation of the universe within.

As your consciousness bursts through the veil of the etheric and sees for the first time the true Light and Sound that represents the touch of Sugmad, the lower processes of the inner – that of the astral, causal, mental and etheric – are energized by the new vibration of the upper frequencies of the Light and Sound. These newly-energized vibrations have been enhanced by the Lords of Karma as a part of the spiritual renaissance taking place. This is the awakening of Soul that has been taking place around the globe. This is the new infusion of the Light and Sound that is being seen in all philosophies of being and ways of life that allow Soul to evolve to its highest form of expression. Beyond this point is where you, as the chosen in The Way of Truth, have been granted a special pathway to the new existence of the Light and Sound that is directly linked to the God Worlds above the Great Divide in accordance with the agreement made by the hierarchies of this Sugmad to bring this universe into alignment with its purpose of generating a new place of existence. For you, the new Sehaji Masters, will carry this message to all those who slumber and remain lost to the lower awareness of the illusion of being set forth in the cycles of reincarnation, guilt and karmic retributions.

The adoption of an understanding of the process of existence in the lower inner worlds of being will help facilitate facsimile alignment – reflective pictures of energy of Soul's past, present and future that exist in both the inner and outer bodies. The wisdom that you have been given access to that is being channeled through the Light and Sound, will allow you to bring this God substance to areas of being below the Great Divide for the first time in this Sugmad. You will become more aware as more is revealed to you in your travels along the sacred ground of the God Worlds, and are allowed to remain in full consciousness of all that you encounter.

All of the lower, inner experiences will be enriched as you bring more new souls into this journey of The Way of Truth, and they will also taste the pure waters of the experience that is yours to share with those willing to match the desire you have shown to be granted this gift of love from Sugmad.

A method by which we can determine the plane of consciousness we are traveling on throughout our day

Your consciousness is replaced as you make every effort to remain in the new alignment of being that is given by the Living Master. Along with this are the directions to access the process of your daily lives through each experience on all planes of awareness. Each level of conscious understanding has its specific purpose as you travel through the daily karmic duties of this Sugmad. With each encounter of freewill, vibrations may become out of balance with the God power that governs your processes. As you wake in the morning, you will retain the instructions that are given in the astral (the dream state) which will balance all that you encounter through the daily activities. The instantaneous response given to the mental body on how to re-balance the cosmic flow will become second nature as you continue to grow through your contemplation and spiritual exercises. Each of the inner planes carries its own specific vibration that is tuned to your quantum, balanced signature, which is aligned with your level of initiatory resonance. Maintaining contact with the inner guidance that is provided to you by those Masters working with you provides the wisdom to wield whatever part of the non-power is necessary to maintain the balance of love that you are growing more and more aware of in your daily lives. This process of being in this consciousness has been passed to you and is recalibrated to respond to your efforts to remain in the selfless open heart attitude of beingness, and will focus the ability to move in a detached manner of goodwill, understanding and always giving the love that Sugmad has placed within you. Cause for concern as to what acts of compassion you may be required to perform are those of the mental body, which,

The Beginning Has No End

The Beginning Has No End

when brought into complete alignment during your morning contemplation, will allow the flow of the Light and Sound to be uninterrupted during the day. Once again, know that it is through the efforts of Dan Rin that you are presented manuals with references to specific contemplative exercises that can increase access to lower inner awareness at any time during your day. (These manuals are available to participants of The Way of Truth).

How we can determine the regular state of consciousness of those we come into contact with in our daily lives

The following discussion enables you to give more guidance about those you encounter in the course of your karmic duties to this Sugmad, and about when to pass the knowledge of the Light and Sound to those that are ready to be awakened. To better understand who is to be brought to this new awareness, you will always be given a sign of willingness that will come from their heart through their words that you will understand as a call from their higher selves that have been nudged by the changed frequencies of the Light and Sound that surrounds you. As you have been placed in this universe to travel this path and to assist in this awakening, you are equipped with the sight of subtle changes in the vibratory fields around people you encounter that are set before you as a task of compassion, and are the ones who are willing to accept the call of this teaching. All of life has the vibration of Sugmad within it, and this is what you have been aligned with to be able to give the connection of the Light and Sound to those who are presented to you. Each heart that comes to you with the openness to take this journey will make itself known to you. The simple words, "I feel that there is something more that I could be doing for myself", will be heard often. Sometimes, in just a simple greeting, you will know that through your eyes shines the true connection to the Light and Sound that carries the love of Sugmad to all that choose to look.

177

Babaji

How we can bless and sanctify our home each and every day

Know that you have walked the sacred ground of the highest consciousness of Sugmad, and that you may wield Its love to protect your home and any ground that you pass over. The open selfless heart allows this flow to be continuous and to repel all that which is not in accordance with the highest laws of Sugmad's love. It is within each of you in your daily lives to also bring this valuable understanding and blessing to those that you may encounter who are in need of this generous gift of the Light and Sound that is so freely given through you.

How we can bring our family and children into a higher state of conscious living

As you work in the grace of Sugmad, there are concentric circles of vibrations that emanate from your higher consciousness that can affect the environment of the home. All those of your family that may not be aware of the Light and Sound that fills the household will still be brought into a harmonious alignment with your higher vibration that infuses into the home the contact of your higher self awareness that guides your efforts to care for those closest to you that you love. Present to them the fact that the singing of the HU will bring a sense of contentment that will soothe them in times of discomfort and will increase the joy that they feel during times of happiness.

The fine balance between love and discipline in the raising of children in our homes

The actions of our children may at times need to be addressed, and at those times always remember that they, too, are graced by the love of Sugmad. As their needs to understand the boundaries of their expression is tested in their actions, know that responding from the middle path, that of detached goodwill, will give a lasting message that they will accept when it comes with the detachment

178

that is filled with love and understanding. Always yielding to the inner guidance as well as the outer knowledge of this world will bring a greater balance to the children as they grow on the outer and the inner. Remember, each of us – regardless of our size, age or awareness – is a soul that is precious to Sugmad and is destined to return once again to Its heart. If a child's behavior is truly perplexing, you may want to check the incarnation scroll of karma to see if the misalignment can be brought into balance through a quantum adjustment in the karmic alignment vibratory range of the Light and Sound, but this would be only in extreme cases.

Why the universe is our home as well

This universe is not only home to us as we see it through our physical senses, but is of great value to use when we travel to its boundaries on the inner in our Universal Soul Movements. We have been placed here for a specific purpose of this Sugmad, and it is best that we take as much care of it as Sugmad has chosen to take care of us. As we begin to travel beyond the boundaries of this universal consciousness, we need to take with us the knowledge and wisdom that we have been blessed with to those we may encounter in other modes of existence that may be outside our immediate understanding.

Why the survival of our culture is dependent on the respect we have toward our elders and the past achievements of those who have preceded us

Our elders carry within their souls the lines of evolvement of the wisdom of how to proceed along this path of growth and expansion. The true nature of wisdom has no way of being maintained except through those of us who are willing to accept the responsibility to keep the sacredness of the love and honor of those that have built this path we now travel. For you to have this chance to travel the realms of beingness that are at your fingertips requires the utmost respect for the forefathers of our search. They have taught those of us who listen with our hearts that our children deserve the same joy that we are afforded, as we search within for the many answers that bring the excitement to our hearts when they are revealed.

Understandings we can give our children on the issues of education, friendship and love

The life that we have been blessed with is a tapestry of experience that covers the walls of ignorance that created the world of illusion. To give to our children the valuable lessons of love and understanding over the thoughts of judgment and misgiving about those things that are strange and unknown, is to never let their hearts be closed to joy and friendship in unlimited amounts. Sharing this great love that fills the heart of true seekers of God's love and wisdom should be given freely in all forms of lessons, so that all children may spend their lives on a much broader path of enlightenment and understanding, than those of us who still struggle in the shadows of illusion and discontentment. To guide them into the values of creativity and higher achievement will enrich the journey toward the spiritual heights that we seek and grow in, within the path that we have traveled.

How we can instruct those under our care and develop greater esteem and unity of character

These questions of teaching have a simple guideline that I offer again and again – there is no greater love that can be given than that of caring in the simplest of ways. If we respect those that we travel with, they will learn to respect themselves. If we give the true love of our selfless connection to God, they will receive the greatest gift imaginable by their own hearts, even if it they are yet to open to the joy of being in love with all creation and becoming aware of their true existence as Soul. Within these mystery teachings of the Light and Sound lies the great path to self-acceptance that can be offered to any that have ever searched within themselves for a place of joy and happiness.

How we can access the negative engrams in our children that will create great challenges in their lives

The spiritual genetic material that has been altered within ourselves has taken us to this new level of God Awareness in which we can live today. As you continue to grow in the ability to wield the non-power in this manifest journey of Soul, it will give to you the ability to infuse into your children the safeguards against the development of negative engrams. When you made the choice to live within the God Consciousness, you generally have built a vibratory shield against the possibility for a child to be led by those things that created in yourself the embryo that formed engrams that may have been negatively charged by your life experiences. As your children grow, the path that may lead them to the life experiences that could produce these engrams will be such that it will present itself to the environment before it can take complete hold upon the lower consciousness of your children. Through your contemplations, these times will be made clear to you through the detached goodwill posture of beingness.

Contemplation I

Here is a contemplative exercise that will give parents skills to develop the necessary levels of introspection within their children, in order for them to survive as spiritually balanced beings in this life

Sit with your children held in the golden light of your selfless beingness.

Bring into your awareness the complete love of Sugmad's heart to protect and cherish them as you do.

Holding this consciousness, begin a **HU** song and continue for as long as you wish.

During the **HU**, see the golden light gently hold them and see it being absorbed into the center of their souls. Within this golden light, infuse the path of the Sacred Heart to unfold in their lives at each juncture of change and/or moments of confusion.

At the end of your **HU**, to safeguard and insure its activation, use this Ancient Egyptian mantra:

TUTRA-TETRAN-TOLTE

The Beginning Has No End

Contemplation II

A contemplative exercise that will give parents the necessary insights into their children's soul contract

It was mentioned before that there may come a time when you may need to access the karmic and/or incarnation records of the child's soul contract. This request must be made of Kusulu for one to be offered an audience before the Red Dragon Order. To be granted this access, it takes the greatest effort of the selfless, detached, transparent posture of heart in Soul. As mentioned before, it is only in extreme cases that such a request may be considered, because the unfoldment of this universe is complex and may carry something beyond the understanding of the caring heart of a parent.

To make this request you must bring the support of the Living Master.

Go into contemplation using your sacred word, then call to Dan Rin to ask for an audience with Kusulu to take your request to the Red Dragon Order for consideration.

You will be asked to remain in the detached open heart consciousness so that there is complete clarity in viewing the scrolls.

The mantra **SOL-TIG-NUM-SAT-LO** was given to afford this consciousness in times of life challenges. Say this mantra three times slowly at the end of the contemplation to afford spiritual protection to the child.

TUTRA-TETRAN-TOLTE

This will insure the spiritual growth of your child with whatever the outcome may be.

Babaji

The Beginning Has No End

INDEX

A

Abuja, Nigeria, 8
Affection
    Personal, 80
African renaissance, 5
Art, 60
Astral 34, 78, 86, 95, 174-176
    Body, 39-40, 119, 145
    Plane, 32-33, 173-174, 188
    Trap, 16
Atlantis, 144
Attitude, 21
Awareness, 77

B

Babaji, i, ii, iii, 5, 8, 62, 134,
    136-137, 165
    Karma and burdens, 165
    Life contract, 165
Balance, 7, 17-18, 21, 30, 37, 42,
    45, 49-50, 65, 76-78, 80, 99,
    109, 133, 137, 156, 166, 176,
    179
    Cosmic, 66, 96, 132, 144
    Cosmic forces, 133
    Cosmic scheme, 107
    Imbalance, 31, 66, 157
    In universe, 97, 155
    Laws of, 78
    Rebalance, 34, 50, 110
    Universal Laws of, 81
    Universe,157
Brakosani, 34, 98
Buddha, 51

C

Care and Caring, 24, 40,

Care and Caring continued:
    44-46, 48, 53, 66-68, 75, 86,
    89, 96-97, 100, 135, 144,
    147-148, 150-152, 163, 180
Causal, 16, 34, 76, 78, 86, 95-96,
    107-108, 118, 151, 158, 175
    Body, 32, 39-40, 59, 147
    Plane, 32, 36, 45, 59, 109, 119,
    173-174
Child Rearing, 178
Children Understanding issues, 180
Christ, 51
Consciousness, i, ii, iii, 6, 14-16,
    18, 20-24, 26, 30-31, 33-40, 42,
    44-50, 52, 54, 58-61, 66-67, 69-
    70, 72-73, 78-80, 84, 87-88, 90-
    92, 94, 97, 99-102, 104, 107-
    108, 110-113, 118-120, 122-
    125, 127, 133-134, 137, 141,
    143, 148-155, 157-159, 163-
    164, 169-171, 173-174, 180-
    186, 188, 190-191, 197-198
    Heart, 144
    God, 147
    Lower, 100
    Spiritual, 76
    Universal, 47, 120, 138
Contemplation(s) 30, 58, 75, 77,
    86, 99, 117-118, 131, 177
    Exercises, 177
Contract and Contracts
    Child's Soul, 183
    Life, 133, 152, 161-162
    Soul, 41, 238

D

Dali Lama, 111
Dan Rin, 16, 19, 22, 24, 30, 34-37,
    40, 42, 50, 52, 59, 88, 97, 99,
    138, 167, 177, 183, *See* Sri
    Michael Owens

185

The Beginning Has No End

V

W

Other Books By
Michael Edward Owens
(Sri Michael Owens)

The Way of Truth Eternal

~ Book I ~

ANCIENT TEACHINGS OF THE
LIGHT AND SOUND OF
GOD
HOW TO LIVE LIFE IN THE GOD WORLDS

MICHAEL EDWARD OWENS

The Way of Truth Eternal
~ Book I ~

The ancient words of truth are written in the sacred pages of the Holy Books of the Light and Sound. These sacred writings are contained and housed and held and protected in sacred temples of light where they are guarded by the members of the Sehaji Hierarchies. As the universe unfolds and progresses, these works are given and revealed in physical form below to create a grounding point for the vortex of their energy and power so that it might be found and felt and experienced within the realms where it is needed.

And so, this is the first of these luminous works given to man by the hand of the Sehaji, Dan Rin, the current Living Sehaji Master, and its words and truth are vital because they do address of critical points of confluence, which previously had been blocked and obstructed and had prevented the clear flows of energy that are necessary and required by those groups of Souls currently incarnated on earth and within the other realms and seeking in their progression to move together onward on the path.

And so, The Way of Truth Eternal, Book I has been sent and given to all Souls to open up their hearts and to aid their understanding and their movement on the path and return to higher realms above.

EKERE TERE
CITY OF LIGHT

This book is a compilation of my spiritual studies with various teachers who are now teaching at Ekere Tere, the City of Light. This city was constructed in the High Astral Plane above the capital city of Abuja, Nigeria. Ekere Tere is a place of learning, specifically designed to forefront the newly calibrated teachings of The Way of Truth, to eradicate the imbalanced presence of black magic in the world and to open the spiritual doors of Africa's Renaissance.

The Way of Truth, the new path of the Light and Sound, stands as the spiritual guardian of all ways of life through the higher learning of Ekere Tere, the City of Light. The Way of Truth affirms the vibratory essence of the Light and Sound in every theology and life-path that holds unconditional love and non-judgment as its foundation. The unitary consciousness of all life is cohesively welded together by Sugmad's love and it is this love which is serving all life as the driving force of existence. It is our heart and its ability to connect with the eternal fabric of Sugmad's plan that opens our Universal Soul Movement to the inexplicable bliss beyond the ken of human eyes. Our heart is the key.

There are many paths to God and each soul must choose the course of their own spiritual unfoldment. This is Soul's eternal right. Soul was placed in a physical shell to understand its immortal gift of existence and to learn in a human laboratory of communication and cooperation, and ultimately to expand its consciousness of love and begin its Universal Soul Movement home.

Within the contents of this book, there is spoken dialogue which presents limitless knowledge to the seekers who want God-Realization in this lifetime. The spoken word of these Masters gives the reader a great opportunity to partake of the love I felt throughout the years of my spiritual training. It is my hope you will try the spiritual exercises to see if they fulfill your spiritual needs. To those seeking to see and visit Ekere Tere, you have my love and Darshan. A great adventure awaits each of you.

Sri Michael Owens